Pocket
Prague

David Bouck
Prague
Salmoska 11
(42)(02) 299-328

(42)(02)

Reprinted from *Fodor's Eastern and Central Europe*

Fodor's Travel Publications, Inc.
New York • Toronto • London • Sydney • Auckland
http://www.fodors.com/

Fodor's Pocket Prague

Editors: Matthew Lore, Glen Berger
Editorial Contributors: Steven K. Amsterdam, Robert Andrews, Mark Baker, Robert Blake, David Brown, Audra Epstein, Charlie Hornberger, Ky Krauthamer, Martha Lagace, Heide Sarna, Helayne Schiff, Mary Ellen Schultz, M. T. Schwartzman (Gold Guide editor), Dinah Spritzer
Creative Director: Fabrizio La Rocca
Associate Art Director: Guido Caroti
Photo Researcher: Jolie Novak
Cartographer: David Lindroth, Inc.
Cover Photograph: Ellen Rooney/International Stock
Text Design: Between the Covers

Copyright

Copyright © 1997 by Fodor's Travel Publications, Inc.

Fodor's is a registered trademark of Fodor's Travel Publications, Inc.

All rights reserved under International and Pan-American Copyright Conventions. Published in the United States by Fodor's Travel Publications, Inc., a subsidiary of Random House, Inc., New York, and simultaneously in Canada by Random House of Canada, Limited, Toronto. Distributed by Random House, Inc., New York.

No maps, illustrations, or other portions of this book may be reproduced in any form without written permission from the publisher.

Second Edition

ISBN 0-679-03272-X

Special Sales

Fodor's Travel Publications are available at special discounts for bulk purchases for sales promotions or premiums. Special editions, including personalized covers, excerpts of existing guides, and corporate imprints, can be created in large quantities for special needs. For more information, contact your local bookseller or write to Special Marketing, Fodor's Travel Publications, 201 E. 50th St., New York, NY 10022; Random House of Canada, Ltd., Marketing Dept., 1265 Aerowood Dr., Mississauga, Ontario L4W 1B9; Fodor's Travel Publications, 20 Vauxhall Bridge Rd., London SW1V 2SA, England.

PRINTED IN THE UNITED STATES OF AMERICA

10 9 8 7 6 5 4 3 2 1

CONTENTS

On the Road with Fodor's — vi

About Our Writers *vi*
On the Web *vi*
New and Noteworthy *vi*
How to Use This Book *vii*
Please Write to Us *viii*

Essential Information — xvi

Important Contacts *xvii*
Smart Travel Tips *xxiv*

1 Destination: Prague — 1

Catching Up to the Present *2*
Pleasures and Pastimes *4*

2 Exploring Prague — 7

Old Town *9*
The Jewish Ghetto *22*
Charles Bridge and Malá Strana *26*
The Castle District *35*
Letná and Holešovice *39*
Vinohrady *41*
Prague Castle *42*

3 Dining — 53

4 Lodging — 62

5 Nightlife and the Arts — 70

6 Shopping — 76

Czech Vocabulary — 80

Index — 88

Maps

Prague *x–xi*
Czech Republic *xii–xiii*
Prague Metro *xiv–xv*
Exploring Prague *10–11*
Prague Castle (Pražský hrad) *44*
Prague Dining *56–57*
Prague Lodging *66–67*

ON THE ROAD WITH FODOR'S

W E'RE ALWAYS thrilled to get letters from readers, especially one like this:

It took us an hour to decide what book to buy and we now know we picked the best one. Your book was wonderful, easy to follow, very accurate, and good on pointing out eating places, informal as well as formal. When we saw other people using your book, we would look at each other and smile.

Our editors and writers are deeply committed to making every Fodor's guide "the best one"—not only accurate but always charming, brimming with sound recommendations and solid ideas, right on the mark in describing restaurants and hotels, and full of fascinating facts that make you view what you've traveled to see in a rich new light.

About Our Writers

Our success in achieving our goals—and in helping to make your trip the best of all possible vacations—is a credit to the hard work of our extraordinary writers and editors. A few of them deserve special mention:

A resident of Prague since 1992, **Ky Krauthamer** is the assistant features editor of the weekly *Prague Post*; he has also contributed to *Fodor's Eastern and Central Europe*, *Fodor's Europe*, and *Fodor's Affordable Europe*. **Martha Lagace** is an editor on the arts and entertainment desk of the *Prague Post*. She grew up in New England, Montana, and Canada, and was a freelance journalist in New York City and Paris before moving to Prague in the spring of 1991. She has also contributed to *Fodor's Eastern and Central Europe*.

On the Web

Check out Fodor's Web site (http://www.fodors.com/), where you'll find travel information on major destinations around the world and an ever-changing array of interactive features.

New and Noteworthy

The Czech Republic continues along its path of economic and cultural revitalization, which began with the peaceful revolution of 1989 and accelerated following the breakup of the Czechoslovak state in 1993. Far from hurting the country, the Czech-Slovak split has freed officials to concentrate on the rapid economic changes of Bohemia and Moravia, without having to worry about Slovakia. Their eventual goal is incorporation into the European Union (EU) by the year 2000. Tourism remains one of the brightest sectors of the economy, and visitors from the West will find the country is still quite affordable. Everywhere, castles, palaces and dusty old museums are spiffing themselves up and throwing open their doors to visitors.

One tangible impact of the country's economic reforms has been an acceleration in the pace of architectural renovations. Many hotels, old private houses, and churches are installing new fixtures and applying a fresh coat of paint. One of the areas to get a face-lift over the past few years is Staroměstské náměstí (Old Town Square), one of the jewels of the "new" Prague, lined by such landmarks as the Týn Church and the Old Town Hall. Brightly painted facades and gleaming shop fronts now fan out from Old Town Square in all directions; the change will astonish visitors who last saw the city as recently as the early 1990s.

The number of hotels and restaurants keeps pace with the growing number of visitors. This is even true of Prague, which has become one of Europe's leading tourist destinations. Like the number of new large hotels, the number of smaller, privately owned hotels and pensions is also on the rise. The arrival of visitors and long-term residents from all over the world has brought forth new restaurants offering Cajun, Mexican, vegetarian, and other exotic fare alongside the traditional ones serving pork and dumplings.

Prague's cultural life continues to thrive and the city in particular is a classical-music lover's dream, with a plethora of concerts to choose from almost every hour of the day in high season. Opera fans should also not be disappointed. The annual mid-May–early June Prague Spring Music Festival, which even before the collapse of the Communist government was one of the great events on the European calendar, is attracting record numbers of music lovers.

How to Use This Book

Organization

Up front is **Essential Information**. Its first section, **Important Contacts**, gives addresses and telephone numbers of organizations and companies that offer destination-related services and detailed information and publications. **Smart Travel Tips**, the second section, gives specific information on how to accomplish what you need to in Prague as well as tips on savvy traveling. Both sections are in alphabetical order by topic.

The Exploring chapter is subdivided by neighborhood with sights listed alphabetically. The chapters that follow are arranged in alphabetical order by subject (dining, lodging, nightlife and the arts, and shopping.

At the end of the book you'll find suggestions for pretrip reading, both fiction and nonfiction, as well as a helpful vocabulary section covering key phrases in Czech.

Icons and Symbols

★ Our special recommendations
✕ Restaurant
🏨 Lodging establishment
🐤 Good for kids (rubber duckie)
☞ Sends you to another section of the guide for more information
✉ Address
☎ Telephone number
☉ Opening and closing times
💰 Admission prices (those we give apply only to adults; substantially reduced fees are almost always available for children, students, and senior citizens)

Hotel Facilities

We always list the facilities that are available—but we don't specify whether they cost extra: When pricing accommodations, always ask what's included.

Restaurant Reservations and Dress Codes

Reservations are always a good idea; we note only when they're essential or when they are not accepted. Book as far ahead as you can, and reconfirm when you get to town. Unless otherwise noted, the restaurants listed are open daily for lunch and dinner. We mention dress only when men are required to wear a jacket or a jacket and tie.

Credit Cards

The following abbreviations are used: **AE,** American Express; **D,** Discover; **DC,** Diners Club; **MC,** MasterCard; and **V,** Visa.

Please Write to Us

You can use this book in the confidence that all prices and opening times are based on information supplied to us at press time; Fodor's cannot accept responsibility for any errors. Time inevitably brings changes, so always confirm information when it matters—especially if you're making a detour to visit a specific place. In addition, when making reservations be sure to mention if you have a disability or are traveling with children, if you prefer a private bath or a certain type of bed, or if you have specific dietary needs or any other concerns.

Were the restaurants we recommended as described? Did our hotel picks exceed your expectations? Did you find a museum we recommended a waste of time? If you have complaints, we'll look into them and revise our entries when the facts warrant it. If you've discovered a special place that we haven't included, we'll pass the information along to our correspondents and have them check it out. So send your feedback, positive *and* negative, to the Eastern and Central Europe editor at 201 East 50th Street, New York, New York 10022—and have a wonderful trip!

Karen Cure
Editorial Director

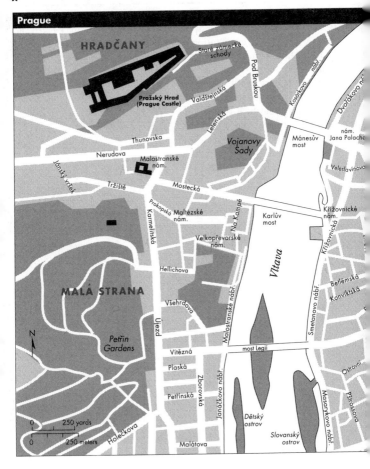

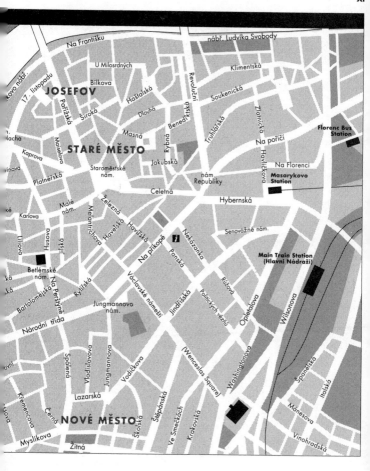

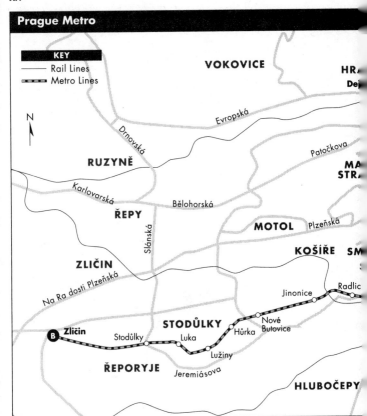

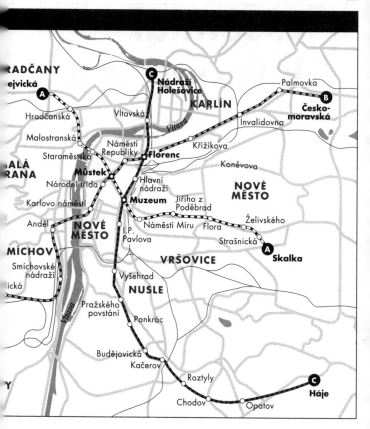

Essential Information

IMPORTANT CONTACTS

An Alphabetical Listing of Publications, Organizations, and Companies That Will Help You Before, During, and After Your Trip

AIR TRAVEL

The major gateway to Prague is **Ruzyne Airport** (☎ 011-42-2/367760), about 32 kilometers (20 miles) northwest of the city.

FLYING TIME

From New York, a nonstop flight to Prague takes 9–10 hours; with a stopover, the journey will take at least 12–13 hours. From Montréal nonstop it is 7½ hours; from Los Angeles, 16 hours.

CARRIERS

Czech Airlines (ČSA, ☎ 212/765-6022) is the only airline that has nonstop flights to Prague from the United States. For connecting flights aboard U.S. carriers, contact **Continental** (☎ 800/231-0856), **Delta** (☎ 800/241-4141), and **United** (☎ 800/538-2929). You'll need to change planes in Europe, and a European airline may operate the last leg of your flight into Prague. Several other international airlines have good connections from cities in the United States and Canada to European bases and from there to Prague. **British Airways** (☎ 800/247-9297) flies daily via London; and **SwissAir** (☎ 800/221-4780), daily via Zurich.

FROM THE U.K.

British Airways (☎ 0181/897-4000 or 0345/222-11 outside London) has daily nonstop service to Prague from London (with connections to major British cities); **ČSA** (☎ 0171/255-1898) flies five times a week nonstop from London. The flight takes around three hours.

AIRPORT TRANSFERS

Between the Airport and Downtown: The Cedaz minibus shuttle links the airport with Náměstí Republiky (a square just off the Old Town). It runs hourly, more often at peak periods, between 6 AM and 9:30 PM daily and makes an intermediate stop at the Dejvická metro station. The one-way fare is 60 Kč. Regular municipal bus service (Bus 119) also connects the airport and the Dejvická metro stop; the fare is 10 Kč. From Dejvická you can take a subway to the city center. To reach Wenceslas Square, get off at the Můstek station.

Taxis offer the easiest and most convenient way of getting downtown. The trip is a straight shot down Evropská Boulevard and takes approximately 20 minutes. The road is not usually busy, but anticipate an additional 20 minutes during rush hour (7–9 AM and 3–6 PM). The ride costs about 300 Kč.

DISABILITIES & ACCESSIBILITY

ORGANIZATIONS

TRAVELERS WITH HEARING IMPAIRMENTS➤ The **American Academy of Otolaryngology** (⊠ 1 Prince St., Alexandria, VA 22314, ☎ 703/836–4444, FAX 703/683–5100, TTY 703/519–1585) publishes a brochure, "Travel Tips for Hearing Impaired People."

TRAVELERS WITH MOBILITY PROBLEMS➤ Contact the **Society for the Advancement of Travel for the Handicapped** (⊠ 347 5th Ave., Suite 610, New York, NY 10016, ☎ 212/447–7284, FAX 212/725–8253; membership $45) and **Travelin' Talk** (⊠ Box 3534, Clarksville, TN 37043, ☎ 615/552–6670, FAX 615/552–1182), which provides local contacts worldwide for travelers with disabilities.

TRAVELERS WITH VISION IMPAIRMENTS➤ Contact the **American Council of the Blind** (⊠ 1155 15th St. NW, Suite 720, Washington, DC 20005, ☎ 202/467–5081, FAX 202/467–5085) for a list of travelers' resources or the **American Foundation for the Blind** (⊠ 11 Penn Plaza, Suite 300, New York, NY 10001, ☎ 212/502–7600 or 800/232–5463, TTY 212/502–7662), which provides general advice and publishes "Access to Art" ($19.95), a directory of museums that accommodate travelers with vision impairments.

IN THE U.K.

Contact the **Royal Association for Disability and Rehabilitation** (⊠ RADAR, 12 City Forum, 250 City Rd., London EC1V 8AF, ☎ 0171/250–3222) or **Mobility International** (⊠ rue de Manchester 25, B-1080 Brussels, Belgium, ☎ 00–322–410–6297, FAX 00–322–410–6874), an international travel-information clearinghouse for people with disabilities.

EMBASSIES

United States (⊠ Tržiště 15, Malá Strana, ☎ 02/2451–0847). **United Kingdom** (⊠ Thunovská ul. 14, Malá Strana, ☎ 02/2451–0439). **Canada** (⊠ Mickiewiczova ul. 6, Hradčany, ☎ 02/2431–1108).

EMERGENCIES

Police (☎ 158). **Ambulance** (☎ 155). **Medical emergencies: Foreigners' Department of Na Homolce Hospital** (⊠ Roentgenova 2, Prague 5, weekdays ☎ 02/5292–2146, evenings and weekends ☎ 02/520022 or 02/5292–2191); **First Medical Clinic of Prague** (⊠ Vyšehradská 35, Prague 2, ☎ 02/292286, 298978; 24-hr emergency ☎ 02/0601–225050, mobile phone). Be prepared to pay in cash for medical treatment, whether you are insured or not. **Dentists** (⊠ Vladislavova 22, Prague 1, ☎ 02/2422–7663 for 24-hr emergency service).

Lost credit cards: American Express (☎ 02/2421–9992); Diners Club, Visa (☎ 02/2412–5353); MasterCard (☎ 02/2442–3135).

GAY & LESBIAN TRAVEL

ORGANIZATIONS

The **International Gay Travel Association** (✉ Box 4974, Key West, FL 33041, ☎ 800/448–8550, FAX 305/296–6633), a consortium of more than 1,000 travel companies, can supply names of gay-friendly travel agents, tour operators, and accommodations.

HEALTH

FINDING A DOCTOR

For its members, the **International Association for Medical Assistance to Travellers** (IAMAT, membership free; ✉ 417 Center St., Lewiston, NY 14092, ☎ 716/754–4883; ✉ 40 Regal Rd., Guelph, Ontario N1K 1B5, ☎ 519/836–0102; ✉ 1287 St. Clair Ave. W, Toronto, Ontario M6E 1B8, ☎ 416/652–0137; ✉ 57 Voirets, 1212 Grand-Lancy, Geneva, Switzerland, no phone) publishes a worldwide directory of English-speaking physicians meeting IAMAT standards.

LATE-NIGHT PHARMACIES

There are two 24-hour pharmacies close to the city's center, both called **Lékárna** (✉ Štefánikova 6, Prague 5, ☎ 02/537039; ✉ Belgická 37, Prague 2, ☎ 02/258189).

INSURANCE

IN THE U.S.

Travel insurance covering baggage, health, and trip cancellation or interruptions is available from **Access America** (✉ 6600 W. Broad St., Richmond, VA 23230, ☎ 804/285–3300 or 800/334–7525), **Carefree Travel Insurance** (✉ Box 9366, 100 Garden City Plaza, Garden City, NY 11530, ☎ 516/294–0220 or 800/323–3149), and **Tele-Trip** (✉ Mutual of Omaha Plaza, Box 31716, Omaha, NE 68131, ☎ 800/228–9792).

IN CANADA

Contact **Mutual of Omaha** (✉ Travel Division, 500 University Ave., Toronto, Ontario M5G 1V8, ☎ 416/598-4083; in Canada, 800/465–0267).

IN THE U.K.

The **Association of British Insurers** (✉ 51 Gresham St., London EC2V 7HQ, ☎ 0171/600–3333) gives advice by phone and publishes the free pamphlet "Holiday Insurance and Motoring Abroad," which sets out typical policy provisions and costs.

MONEY

ATMS

For specific foreign **Cirrus** locations, call 800/424–7787; for foreign **Plus** locations, consult the Plus directory at your local bank.

PASSPORTS & VISAS

IN THE U.S.
For fees, documentation requirements, and other information, call the State Department's **Office of Passport Services** information line (☎ 202/647–0518).

IN CANADA
For fees, documentation requirements, and other information, call the Ministry of Foreign Affairs and International Trade's **Passport Office** (☎ 819/994–3500 or 800/567–6868).

IN THE U.K.
For fees, documentation requirements, and to request an emergency passport, call the **London Passport Office** (☎ 0990/210410).

SENIOR CITIZENS

EDUCATIONAL TRAVEL
Interhostel (✉ University of New Hampshire, 6 Garrison Ave., Durham, NH 03824, ☎ 603/862–1147 or 800/733–9753), for travelers 50 and older, has two- to three-week trips; most last two weeks and cost $2,000–$3,500, including airfare.

ORGANIZATIONS
Contact the **American Association of Retired Persons** (✉ AARP, 601 E St. NW, Washington, DC 20049, ☎ 202/434–2277; annual dues $8 per person or couple). Its Purchase Privilege Program secures discounts for members on lodging, car rentals, and sightseeing.

STUDENTS

HOSTELING
In the United States, contact **Hostelling International–American Youth Hostels** (✉ 733 15th St. NW, Suite 840, Washington, DC 20005, ☎ 202/783–6161, FAX 202/783–6171); in Canada, **Hostelling International–Canada** (✉ 205 Catherine St., Suite 400, Ottawa, Ontario K2P 1C3, ☎ 613/237–7884); and in the United Kingdom, the **Youth Hostel Association of England and Wales** (✉ Trevelyan House, 8 St. Stephen's Hill, St. Albans, Hertfordshire AL1 2DY, ☎ 01727/855215 or 01727/845047). Membership (in the U.S., $25; in Canada, C$26.75; in the U.K., £9.30) gives you access to 5,000 hostels in 77 countries that charge $5–$40 per person per night.

ORGANIZATIONS
A major contact is the **Council on International Educational Exchange** (✉ Mail orders only: CIEE, 205 E. 42nd St., 16th floor, New York, NY 10017, ☎ 212/822–2600, FAX 212/822–2699, info@ciee.org).

TELEPHONES

The country code for the Czech Republic is 42. For local access numbers abroad, contact **AT&T** USADirect (☎ 800/874–4000), **MCI** Call USA (☎ 800/444–4444), or **Sprint** Express (☎ 800/793–1153).

TOUR OPERATORS

Among the companies that sell tours and packages to Prague, the following are nationally known, have a proven reputation, and offer plenty of options.

GROUP TOURS

SUPER-DELUXE➤ **Abercrombie & Kent** (⊠ 1520 Kensington Rd., Oak Brook, IL 60521-2141, ☎ 708/954-2944 or 800/323-7308, FAX 708/954-3324) and **Travcoa** (⊠ Box 2630, 2350 S.E. Bristol St., Newport Beach, CA 92660, ☎ 714/476-2800 or 800/992-2003, FAX 714/476-2538).

DELUXE➤ **Tauck Tours** (⊠ Box 5027, 276 Post Rd. W, Westport, CT 06881, ☎ 203/226-6911 or 800/468-2825, FAX 203/221-6828).

FIRST CLASS➤ **Cedok Travel** (⊠ 10 E. 40th St., #3604, New York, NY 10016, ☎ 212/725-0948 or 800/800-8891) and **General Tours** (⊠ 53 Summer St., Keene, NH 03431, ☎ 603/357-5033 or 800/221-2216, FAX 603/357-4548).

PACKAGES

Independent vacation packages that include round-trip airfare and hotel accommodations are available from major airlines and tour operators. Among U.S. carriers, contact **Delta Dream Vacations** (☎ 800/872-7786) and **United Vacations** (☎ 800/328-6877). Leading tour operators include **Central Holidays** (⊠ 206 Central Ave., Jersey City, NJ 07307, ☎ 201/798-5777 or 800/935-5000), **DER Tours** (⊠ 11933 Wilshire Blvd., Los Angeles, CA 90025, ☎ 310/479-4140 or 800/937-1235) and **General Tours** (☞ Group Tours, *above*).

FROM THE U.K.

Contact **British Airways Holidays** (⊠ Astral Towers, Betts Way, London Rd., Crawley, West Sussex RH10 2XA, ☎ 01293/723-100), **Travelscene** (⊠ Travelscene House, 11-15 St. Ann's Rd., Harrow, Middlesex HA1 1AS, ☎ 0181/427-8800), or **Sovereign** (⊠ First Choice House, Peel Cross Rd., Salford, Manchester M5 2AN, ☎ 0161/742-2244).

THEME TRIPS

Travel Contacts (⊠ Box 173, Camberley, GU15 1YE, England, ☎ 1/27667-7217, FAX 1/2766-3477), which represents 150 tour operators, can satisfy just about any special interest in Prague.

ART AND ARCHITECTURE➤ For educational programs in Prague, contact **Smithsonian Study Tours and Seminars** (⊠ 1100 Jefferson Dr. SW, Room 3045, MRC 702, Washington, DC 20560, ☎ 202/357-4700, FAX 202/633-9250).

BALLOONING➤ **Buddy Bombard European Balloon Adventures** (⊠ 855 Donald Ross Rd., Juno

Beach, FL 33408, ☎ 407/775–0039 or 800/862–8537, FAX 407/775–7008) operates balloon holidays in Prague.

BARGE/RIVER CRUISES➤ Contact **KD River Cruises of Europe** (⊠ 2500 Westchester Ave., Purchase, NY 10577, ☎ 914/696–3600 or 800/346–6525, FAX 914/696–0833) for trips on the Elbe River between Dresden and Prague.

HISTORY➤ History buffs should contact **Herodot Travel** (⊠ 775 E. Blithedale, Box 234, Mill Valley, CA 94941, ☎ FAX 415/381–4031).

JUDAISM➤ Jewish life in Prague is the subject of a tour from the **American Jewish Congress** (⊠ 15 E. 84th St., New York, NY 10028, ☎ 212/879–4588 or 800/221–4694).

LEARNING VACATIONS➤ **Smithsonian Study Tours and Seminars** (☞ Art and Architecture, *above*).

PERFORMING ARTS➤ **Dailey-Thorp Travel** (⊠ 330 W. 58th St., #610, New York, NY 10019-1817, ☎ 212/307–1555 or 800/998–4677, FAX 212/974–1420) specializes in classical-music and opera programs in Prague.

TRAIN TRAVEL

For train times, consult timetables in stations or get in line at the information offices upstairs at the main station, open daily 6 AM–10 PM, or downstairs near the exits (under the ČD Centrum sign), or call 02/2422–4200. The Čedok office at Na příkopě 18 (☎ 02/2419–7111) also provides train information and issues tickets.

TRANSPORTATION WITHIN PRAGUE

BY BUS

The Czech complex of regional bus lines known collectively as **ČSAD** operates its dense network from the sprawling main bus station on Křižíkova (metro stop: Florenc, Line B or C). For information about routes and schedules call 02/2421–1060, consult the confusingly displayed timetables posted at the station, or visit the information window, situated at the bus unloading area (☉ Weekdays 6–7:45, Sat. 6–4, Sun. 8–6). The helpful private travel agency Tourbus, in the pedestrian overpass above the station, dispenses bus information daily until 8 PM. If the ticket windows are closed, you can usually buy a ticket from the driver.

BY CAR

Don't rent a car if you intend to visit only Prague. Most of the center of the city is closed to traffic, and you'll save yourself a lot of hassle by sticking to public transportation.

From the United States: **Avis** (☎ 800/331–1084; in Canada, 800/879–2847), **Budget** (☎ 800/527–0700; in the U.K., 0800/181181), **Hertz** (☎ 800/654–3001; in Canada, 800/263–0600; in the U.K., 0345/555888).

In Prague: **Avis** (✉ Elišky Krásnohorské 9, Prague 7, ☎ 02/231–5515), **Budget** (✉ Hotel Inter-Continental, ☎ 02/2488–9995), **Hertz** (✉ Karlovo náměstí 28, Prague 2, ☎ 297836 or 290122).

BY TAXI

Two reputable firms are **AAA Taxi** (☎ 02/3399) and **Sedop** (☎ 02/6731–4184).

TRAVEL AGENCIES

For names of reputable agencies in your area, contact the **American Society of Travel Agents** (✉ ASTA, 1101 King St., Suite 200, Alexandria, VA 22314, ☎ 703/739–2782), the **Association of Canadian Travel Agents** (✉ Suite 201, 1729 Bank St., Ottawa, Ontario K1V 7Z5, ☎ 613/521–0474, FAX 613/521–0805), or the **Association of British Travel Agents** (✉ 55–57 Newman St., London W1P 4AH, ☎ 0171/637–2444, FAX 0171/637–0713).

VISITOR INFORMATION

Čedok (Czech Travel Bureau and Tourist Office, ✉ 10 E. 40th St., New York, NY 10016, ☎ 212/689–9720, FAX 212/481–0597; in the U.K.: ✉ 49 Southwark St., London SE1 1RU, ☎ 0171/378–6009, FAX 0171/403–2321; in Prague: main office, ✉ Na příkopě 18, ☎ 02/2419–7111, FAX 02/2422–5339, ◷ Weekdays 8:30–6, Sat. 9–1; other downtown offices: ✉ Rytířská 16 and Pařížská 6), the ubiquitous travel agency, is the first stop for general tourist information and city maps. Čedok will also exchange money, arrange guided tours, and book passage on airlines, buses, and trains. You can pay for Čedok services, including booking rail tickets, with any major credit card.

The Prague Information Service (PIS) (In Prague: ✉ Staroměstské nám. 22, and Na příkopě 20) is generally less helpful than Čedok but offers city maps and general tourist information and arranges group and individual tours. It can also exchange money and help in obtaining tickets for cultural events.

The **Czech Tourist Authority** (In Prague: ✉ Národní třída 37, ☎ FAX 02/2421–1458) can provide information on tourism outside Prague, but does not sell tickets or book accommodations.

Also contact the **Czech Republic Tourist Board** (in the U.S. and Canada: ✉ 1109 Madison Ave., New York, NY 10028, ☎ 212/288–0830) and the **Czech Center** (In the U.S. and Canada: ✉ 1109 Madison Ave., NewYork, NY 10028, ☎ 212/288–0830; in the U.K.: ✉ 49 Southwark St., London SE1 1RU, ☎ 0171/378–6009, FAX 0171/403–2321; ✉ 30 Kensington Palace Gardens, London W8 4QY, ☎ 0171/243–7981, FAX 0171/727–9589).

SMART TRAVEL TIPS

Basic Information on Traveling in Prague and Savvy Tips to Make Your Trip a Breeze

AIR TRAVEL

Ruzyně Airport: Situated 20 kilometers (12 miles) northwest of the downtown area, the airport is small but easily negotiated; **allow yourself plenty of time when departing Prague,** because the airport is still too small to handle the large numbers of travelers who move through it, and you may encounter long lines at customs and check-in.

CUSTOMS & DUTIES

To speed your clearance through customs, **keep receipts for all your purchases abroad** and **be ready to show the inspector what you've bought.** If you feel that you've been incorrectly or unfairly charged a duty, you can **appeal assessments in dispute.** First ask to see a supervisor. If you are still unsatisfied, **write to the port director** at your point of entry, sending your customs receipt and any other appropriate documentation. The address will be listed on your receipt. If you still don't get satisfaction, you can take your case to customs headquarters in Washington.

IN PRAGUE

You may import duty-free into the Czech Republic 250 cigarettes or the equivalent in tobacco, 1 liter of spirits, and 2 liters of wine. In addition to the above, you are permitted to import gifts valued at up to 1,000 Kčs (approximately $35).

If you are bringing into any of these countries any valuables or foreign-made equipment from home, such as cameras, it's wise to carry the original receipts with you or register the items with U.S. Customs before you leave (Form 4457). Otherwise you could end up paying duty upon your return..

IN THE U.S.

You may bring home $400 worth of foreign goods duty-free if you've been out of the country for at least 48 hours and haven't already used the $400 allowance, or any part of it, in the past 30 days.

Travelers 21 or older may bring back 1 liter of alcohol duty-free, provided the beverage laws of the state through which they reenter the United States allow it. In addition, regardless of their age, they are allowed 100 non-Cuban cigars and 200 cigarettes. Antiques, which the U.S. Customs Service defines as objects more than 100 years old, are duty-free. Original works of art done entirely by hand are also duty-free. These include, but are not limited to, paintings, drawings, and sculptures.

Duty-free, travelers may mail packages valued at up to $200 to themselves and up to $100 to others, with a limit of one parcel per addressee per day (and no alcohol or tobacco products or perfume valued at more than $5); on the outside, the package must be labeled as being either for personal use or an unsolicited gift, and a list of its contents and their retail value must be attached. Mailed items do not affect your duty-free allowance on your return.

IN CANADA

If you've been out of Canada for at least seven days, you may bring in C$500 worth of goods duty-free. If you've been away for fewer than seven days but for more than 48 hours, the duty-free allowance drops to C$200; if your trip lasts between 24 and 48 hours, the allowance is C$50. You cannot pool allowances with family members. Goods claimed under the C$500 exemption may follow you by mail; those claimed under the lesser exemptions must accompany you.

Alcohol and tobacco products may be included in the seven-day and 48-hour exemptions but not in the 24-hour exemption. If you meet the age requirements of the province or territory through which you reenter Canada, you may bring in, duty-free, 1.14 liters (40 imperial ounces) of wine or liquor *or* 24 12-ounce cans or bottles of beer or ale. If you are 16 or older, you may bring in, duty-free, 200 cigarettes, 50 cigars or cigarillos, and 400 tobacco sticks or 400 grams of manufactured tobacco. Alcohol and tobacco must accompany you on your return.

An unlimited number of gifts with a value of up to C$60 each may be mailed to Canada duty-free. These do not affect your duty-free allowance on your return. Label the package "Unsolicited Gift—Value Under $60." Alcohol and tobacco are excluded.

IN THE U.K.

From countries outside the European Union, including the Czech Republic, you may import, duty-free, 200 cigarettes, 100 cigarillos, 50 cigars, or 250 grams of tobacco; 1 liter of spirits or 2 liters of fortified or sparkling wine or liqueurs; 2 liters of still table wine; 60 milliliters of perfume; 250 milliliters of toilet water; plus £136 worth of other goods, including gifts and souvenirs.

DISABILITIES & ACCESSIBILITY

Provisions for travelers with disabilities are extremely limited; **traveling with a nondisabled companion is probably the best solution.** While many hotels, especially large American or international chains, offer some wheelchair-accessible rooms, special facilities at museums, restaurants, and on public transportation are difficult to find.

GUIDED TOURS

Čedok (☞ Visitor Information *in* Important Contacts, *above*) sponsors several tours of the city. The three-hour "Historical Prague" tour (✉ 490 Kč), offered year-round, is a combination bus-walking venture that covers all of the major sights. It departs daily at 10 AM and 2 PM from the Čedok office at Pařížská 6 (near the Inter-Continental Hotel). Between May and October, "Panoramic Prague" (✉ 300 Kč), an abbreviated version of the above tour, departs Wednesday, Friday and Saturday at 11 AM from the Čedok office at Na příkopě 18. On Friday Čedok also offers "Prague on Foot," a slower-paced, three-hour walking tour that departs at 9:30 AM from Na příkopě 18. The price is 290 Kč. More tours are offered especially in summer, and the above schedule may well vary according to demand. Prices may also go up in high season.

Many private firms now offer combination bus-walking tours of the city that typically last two or three hours and cost 300 Kč–400 Kč or more. You can also arrange for a personalized walking tour. Times and itineraries are negotiable; prices start at around 500 Kč per hour. For more information, address inquiries to any of the dozen operators with booths on Wenceslas Square, Staroměstské náměstí (near the Jan Hus monument), or Náměstí Republiky (near the Obecní Dům).

HEALTH

You may gain weight, but there are few other serious health hazards for the traveler in the Czech Republic. Tap water tastes bad but is generally drinkable; when it runs rusty out of the tap or the aroma of chlorine is overpowering, it might help to have some iodine tablets or bottled water handy.

To avoid problems clearing customs, diabetic travelers carrying needles and syringes should have on hand a letter from their physician confirming their need for insulin injections.

LANGUAGE

Czech, a Slavic language closely related to Slovak and Polish, is the official language of the Czech Republic. Learning English is popular among young people, but German is still the most useful language for tourists. Don't be surprised if you get a response in German to a question asked in English. If the idea of attempting Czech is daunting, you might consider bringing a German phrase book.

MAIL

Postcards to the United States cost 6 Kč; letters up to 20 grams in weight, 10 Kč; to Great Britain a postcard is 5 Kč; a letter, 8 Kč. You can buy stamps at post offices, hotels, and shops that sell postcards.

MONEY

CURRENCY

The unit of currency in the Czech Republic is the koruna, or crown (Kč), which is divided into 100 haléř, or halers. There are (little-used) coins of 10, 20, and 50 halers; coins of 1, 2, 5, 10, 20, and 50 Kč, and notes of 20, 50, 100, 200, 500, 1,000, and 5,000 Kč. The 1,000-Kč note may not always be accepted for small purchases, because the proprietor may not have enough change.

Try to avoid exchanging money at hotels or private exchange booths, including the ubiquitous Čekobanka and Exact Change booths. They routinely take commissions of 8%–10%. The best place to exchange is at bank counters, where the commissions average 1%–3%, or at ATMs. The *koruna* became fully convertible late in 1995, and can now be purchased outside the country and exchanged into other currencies. Ask about current regulations when you change money, however, and keep your receipts. At press time the exchange rate was around 27 Kč to the U.S. dollar, 19 Kč to the Canadian dollar, and 41 Kč to the pound sterling.

WHAT IT WILL COST

Despite rising inflation, the Czech Republic is still generally a bargain by Western standards. Prague remains the exception, however. Hotel prices, in particular, frequently meet or exceed the average for the United States and Western Europe—and are higher than the standard of facilities would warrant. Nevertheless, you can still find bargain private accommodations. Tourists can now legally pay for hotel rooms in crowns, although some hotels still insist on payment in "hard" (i.e., Western) currency.

SAMPLE COSTS

A cup of coffee will cost about 15 Kč; museum entrance, 20 Kč–150 Kč; a good theater seat, up to 200 Kč; a cinema seat, 30 Kč–50 Kč; ½ liter (pint) of beer, 15 Kč–25 Kč; a 1-mile taxi ride, 60 Kč–100 Kč; a bottle of Moravian wine in a good restaurant, 100 Kč–150 Kč; a glass (2 deciliters or 7 ounces) of wine, 25 Kč.

ATMS

CASH ADVANCES➤ Before leaving home, **make sure that your credit cards have been programmed for ATM use in Prague.** Note that Discover is accepted mostly in the United States. Local bank cards often do not work overseas either; **ask your bank about a MasterCard/Cirrus or Visa debit card,** which works like a bank card but can be used at any ATM displaying a MasterCard/Cirrus or Visa logo.

TRANSACTION FEES➤ Although fees charged for ATM transactions may be higher abroad than at home, Cirrus and Plus exchange rates are excellent, because they are based on wholesale rates offered only by major banks.

NATIONAL HOLIDAYS

January 1; Easter Monday; May 1 (Labor Day); May 8 (Liberation Day); July 5 (Sts. Cyril and Methodius); July 6 (Jan Hus); October 28 (Czech National Day); and December 24, 25, and 26.

OPENING AND CLOSING TIMES

Though hours vary, most banks are open weekdays 8–5, with an hour's lunch break. Private exchange offices usually have longer hours. Museums are usually open daily except Monday (or Tuesday) 9–5; they tend to stop selling tickets an hour before closing time. Outside the large towns, many sights, including most castles, are open daily except Monday only from May through September, and in April and October open only on weekends and holidays. Stores are open weekdays 9–6; some grocery stores open at 6 AM. Department stores often stay open until 7 PM. On Saturday, most stores close at noon. Nearly all stores are closed on Sunday.

PASSPORTS & VISAS

IN THE U.S.

All U.S. citizens, even infants, need only a valid passport to enter the Czech Republic for stays of up to 30 days. Application forms for both first-time and renewal passports are available at any of the 13 U.S. Passport Agency offices and at some post offices and courthouses. Passports are usually mailed within four weeks; allow five weeks or more in spring and summer.

CANADIANS

You need only a valid passport to enter the Czech Republic for stays of up to 30 days. Passport application forms are available at 28 regional passport offices, as well as post offices and travel agencies. Whether for a first or a renewal passport, you must apply in person. Children under 16 may be included on a parent's passport but must have their own to travel alone. Passports are valid for five years and are usually mailed within two to three weeks of application.

U.K. CITIZENS

Citizens of the United Kingdom need only a valid passport to enter the Czech Republic for stays of up to 30 days. Applications for new and renewal passports are available from main post offices and at the passport offices in Belfast, Glasgow, Liverpool, London, Newport, and Peterborough. You may apply in person at all passport offices, or by mail to all except the London office. Children under 16 may travel on an accompanying parent's passport. All passports are valid for 10 years. Allow a month for processing.

TELEPHONES

LOCAL CALLS

The few remaining coin-operated telephones take 1-, 2-, and 5-Kč coins. Most newer public phones operate only with a special telephone card, available from newsstands and tobacconists in denominations of 100 Kč and 190 Kč. A call within Prague costs 2 Kč. The dial tone is a series of short–long buzzes.

INTERNATIONAL CALLS

To reach an English-speaking operator in the United States, dial 00–420–00101 (**AT&T**), 00–420–00112 (**MCI**), or 0420–87187 (**Sprint**). For **CanadaDirect**, dial 00420–00151; for **B.T.Direct** to the United Kingdom, 00420–04401. The operator will connect your collect or credit-card call at the carrier's standard rates. In Prague, many phone booths allow direct international dialing; if you can't find one, the main post office (Hlavní pošta, ✉ Jindřišská ul. 14), open 24 hours, is the best place to try. There you can use the public phones in the lobby or ask one of the clerks in the 24-hour telephone room, to the left as you enter, for assistance. Twenty-four-hour fax and telex service is handled from the office to the right of the entrance. The international dialing code is 00. For international inquiries, dial 0132 for the United States, Canada, or the United Kingdom. Otherwise, ask the receptionist at any hotel to put a call through for you, though beware: The more expensive the hotel, the more expensive the call will be.

TIPPING

To reward good service in a restaurant, round the bill up to the nearest multiple of 10 (if the bill comes to 83 Kč, for example, give the waiter 90 Kč); 10% is considered appropriate on very large tabs. If you have difficulty communicating the amount to the waiter, just leave the money on the table. Tip porters who bring bags to your rooms 20 Kč. For room service, a 20-Kč tip is enough. In taxis, round the bill up by 10%. Give tour guides and helpful concierges between 20 Kč and 30 Kč for services rendered.

TRAIN TRAVEL

International trains arrive at and depart from either the main station, Hlavní nádraží, Wilsonova ulice, about 500 yards east of Wenceslas Square; or the suburban Nádraží Holešovice, situated about 2 kilometers (1½ miles) north of the city center. This is an unending source of confusion—**always make certain you know which station your train is using.**

FROM THE U.K.

There are no direct trains from London. You can take a direct train from Paris via Frankfurt to Prague (daily). There are three trains a day from Vienna's Franz Josefsbahnhof to Prague via Třeboň and Tábor (5½ hours) and one from the Südbahnhof (South Station) via Brno (5 hours).

BETWEEN THE TRAIN STATIONS AND CITY CENTER

Wenceslas Square is a convenient five-minute walk from the main station, or you can take the subway one stop to Muzeum. A taxi ride from the main station to the center will cost about 50 Kč. To reach the city center from Nádraží Holešovice, take the subway (Line C) four stops to Muzeum.

TRANSPORTATION WITHIN PRAGUE

To see Prague properly, there is no alternative to walking, especially since much of the city center is off-limits to automobiles. And the walking couldn't be more pleasant—most of it along the beautiful bridges and cobblestone streets of the city's historic core. Before venturing out, however, **be sure you have a good map.**

BY BUS AND TRAM

Prague's extensive bus and streetcar network allows for fast, efficient travel throughout the city. Tickets are the same as those used for the metro, although you validate them at machines inside the bus or streetcar. Tickets (*jizdenky*) can be bought at hotels, newsstands, and from dispensing machines in the metro stations. The price of a ticket increased in 1996 from 6 Kč to 10 Kč; the new tickets permit one hour's travel throughout the metro, tram, and bus network, rather than the one ticket–one ride system. You can also buy one-day passes allowing unlimited use of the system for 50 Kč, two-day for 85 Kč, three-day for 110 Kč, and five-day for 170 Kč. The passes can be purchased at the main metro stations and at some newsstands. A refurbished old tram, No. 91, plies a route in the Old Town and Lesser Quarter on summer weekends. Trams 50–59 and Buses 500 and above run all night, after the metro shuts down at midnight. All "night tram" routes intersect at the corner of Lazarská and Spálená streets in the New Town near the Národní Třída metro station. **Be on the alert for pickpockets,** who often operate in large groups on crowded trams, buses, and metro cars.

BY CAR

If you are limiting your trip to Prague, **having a car is often more hassle than its worth.** During the day traffic can be heavy, especially on the approach to Wenceslas Square. Pay particular attention to the trams, which enjoy the right-of-way in every situation. Note that parts of the historic center of Prague, including Wenceslas Square itself, are closed to private vehicles.

Parking is permitted in the center of town, including on Wenceslas Square, with a voucher from one of the major hotels, on a growing number of streets with parking meters, or in the few small lots within walking distance of the historic center. An underground lot is at Nám. Jana Palacha, near Old Town Square.

LICENSE REQUIREMENTS➤ In the Czech Republic your own driver's license is acceptable. An International Driver's Permit is a good idea; it's available from the American or Canadian automobile associations, or, in the United Kingdom, from the AA or RAC.

BY SUBWAY

Prague's subway system, the metro, is clean and reliable. Trains run daily from 5 AM to midnight. Validate the tickets at the orange machines before descending the escalators; each ticket is good for 60 minutes of uninterrupted travel. Trains are patrolled often; the fine for riding without a valid ticket is 200 Kč.

BY TAXI

Dishonest taxi drivers are the shame of the nation. Luckily visitors do not need to rely on taxis for trips within the city center (it's usually easier to walk or take the subway). Typical scams include drivers doctoring the meter or simply failing to turn the meter on and then demanding an exorbitant sum at the end of the ride. In an honest cab, the meter will start at 10 Kč and increase by 12 Kč per kilometer (½-mile) or 1 Kč per minute at rest. Most rides within town should cost no more than 80 Kč–100 Kč. To minimize the chances of getting ripped off, avoid taxi stands in Wenceslas Square and other heavily touristed areas. The best alternative is to phone for a taxi in advance. Many firms have English-speaking operators.

VISITOR INFORMATION

To find out what's on for the month and to get the latest tips for shopping, dining, and entertainment, consult Prague's weekly English-language newspaper, the ***Prague Post.*** It prints comprehensive entertainment listings and can be bought at most downtown newsstands as well as in major North American and European cities. The monthly ***Prague Guide,*** available at newsstands and tourist offices for 25 Kč, provides a good overview of major cultural events and has listings of restaurants, hotels, and organizations offering traveler assistance.

1 Destination: Prague

CATCHING UP TO THE PRESENT

"The city was changing."

— Jachým Topol, *A Trip to the Train Station*

AT THE TABLES of a few select pubs in the Smíchov district of Prague, you can occasionally find Jachým Topol, the Czech Republic's most highly prized young novelist and poet, quietly passing away the afternoon hunched in a rickety wooden chair. His literary reputation aside, Topol seems much like any other young Czech who, for one reason or another, passes a weekday afternoon in a corner pub, sipping beer and smoking his way through a pack of Spartas or Petras or some such horrible brand of local cigarettes.

Like many here who divide their time neatly between "pubbing" and working, Topol has produced some of the Czech Republic's most vivid chronicles of late-20th-century, post-Communist society, although his reputation is far less prominent than that of novelists like Ivan Klíma, whose recent novel, *The Judge,* is also among the few "new" pieces of serious literature produced since 1989. One of Topol's more recent novellas, *A Trip to the Train Station,* published locally in a dual-language, Czech-English paperback edition, is a stream-of-consciousness look at the new Prague. It is a fine introduction to a fascinating city: Topol introduces readers to the excited world of black marketeers and concentration camp survivors, incompetent hitmen and journalists on the take, and even takes a poke at the thousands of young Americans who have taken up residence in Prague. Its pages walk the streets of his "city of a thousand faces," passing beneath its baroque and Gothic towers, staring up at the art-nouveau, stained-glass canopy of its main train station, browsing its secondhand bookstores, and strolling past its tiny shops 10-to-a-block.

That multitude of faces and facades—the ones that Jachým says replaced the "mask of rotting Bolshevism"—is perhaps the most fascinating part of the new Eastern and Central Europe. Though the years between World War II and the fall of communism have left a vicious economic and social hangover, Prague is alive with a frenetic brand of commerce, with a rapidly changing and still-young street culture, with jazz trios that play Thelonious Monk, art galleries that exhibit avant-garde conceptualist sculpture, and performances of Mozart's *Don Gio-*

vanni in the same house that saw its premiere two centuries ago.

Prague made its debut as a European metroplis in the 9th century, but spent several hundred years languishing under the dominance of more powerful states. Prague became the political and cultural center of Europe in the 14th century, during the long reign of Charles IV, king of Bohemia and Moravia and Holy Roman Emperor. It was Charles who established Central Europe's first university and laid out the New Town (Nové Město).

During the 15th century, the city's development was hampered by the Hussite Wars, a series of crusades launched by the Holy Roman Empire to subdue the fiercely independent Czech noblemen. The Czechs were eventually defeated in 1620 at the Battle of White Mountain (Bílá Hora) near Prague and were ruled by the Hapsburg family for the next 300 years. Under the Hapsburgs, Prague became a German-speaking city and an important administrative center, but it was forced to play second fiddle to the monarchy's capital of Vienna. Much of the Lesser Town (Malá Strana), across the Vltava River, was built up at this time, becoming home to Austrian nobility and its baroque tastes.

Prague regained its status as a national capital in 1918, with the creation of the modern Czechoslovak state, and quickly asserted itself in the interwar period as a vital cultural center. Although the city escaped World War II essentially intact, it and the rest of Czechoslovakia fell under the political and cultural domination of the Soviet Union until the 1989 popular uprisings. The election of dissident playwright Václav Havel to the post of national president set the stage for the city's renaissance, which has since proceeded at a dizzying, quite Bohemian rate.

Though Prague is now deluged by tourists during the summer months, the sense of history—stretching back through centuries of wars, empires, and monuments to everyday life—remains mostly uncluttered by the trappings of modernity. The peculiar melancholy of Central Europe, less tainted now by the oppressive political realities of the postwar era, still lurks in narrow streets and forgotten corners.

— Charlie Hornberger

PLEASURES AND PASTIMES

Dining

The quality of restaurant cuisine in Prague remains uneven, but many excellent private restaurants have sprung up in recent years. The traditional dishes—roast pork or duck with dumplings, or broiled meat with sauce—can be light and tasty when well prepared.

Restaurants generally fall into three categories. A *pivnice,* or beer hall, usually offers a simple menu of goulash or pork with dumplings at very low prices. In the congenial atmosphere, you can expect to share a table. More attractive (and more expensive) are the *vinárna* (wine cellars) and *restaurace* (restaurants), which serve a full range of dishes. Wine cellars, some occupying Romanesque basements, can be a real treat, and you should certainly seek them out. A fourth dining option, the *lahůdky* (snack bar or deli), is the quickest and cheapest option.

Lunch, usually eaten between noon and 2, is the main meal for Czechs and offers the best deal for tourists. Many restaurants put out a special luncheon menu (*denní lístek*), usually printed only in Czech, with more appetizing selections at better prices. If you don't see it, ask your waiter. Dinner is usually served from 5 until 9 or 10, but don't wait too long to eat. First of all, most Czechs eat only a light meal or a cold plate of meat and cheese in the evening. Second, restaurant cooks frequently knock off early on slow nights, and the later you arrive, the more likely it is that the kitchen will be closed. In general, dinner menus do not differ substantially from lunch offerings, except that the prices are higher.

Lodging

Finding a suitable room should pose no problem, although it is highly recommended that you book ahead during the peak tourist season (July and August, and the Christmas and Easter holidays). Hotel prices, in general, remain high. Better value can often be found at private pensions and with individual homeowners offering rooms to let.

The Czech Republic's official hotel classification now follows the international star system. These ratings correspond closely to our categories as follows: Deluxe or five-star plus four-star ($$$$); three-star ($$$); two-star ($$). Accommodations in the $ category are generally private rooms. Often you can book rooms—both at hotels and in private homes—through Čedok or visitor bureaus.

Otherwise, try calling or writing the hotel directly.

The prices quoted below are for double rooms during high season, generally not including breakfast. At certain periods, such as Easter or during festivals, prices can jump 15%–25%; as a rule, always ask the price before taking a room.

Shopping

Look for elegant and unusual crystal and porcelain. You can also find excellent ceramics, as well as other folk artifacts, such as printed textiles, lace, hand-knit sweaters, and painted eggs. Here you'll also find *Becherovka*, a tasty herbal aperitif that makes a nice gift to take home.

Wine

Best-known as a nation of beer makers, the Czechs also produce quite drinkable wines: peppy, fruity whites and mild, versatile reds. Southern Moravia, with comparatively warm summers and rich soil, grows the bulk of the wine harvest; look for the Mikulov and Znojmo regional designations. Favorite white varietals are **Müller Thurgau,** with a fine muscat bouquet and light flavor that go well with fish and veal, and **Neuburské,** yellow-green in color and with a dry, smoky bouquet, delicious with roasts. **Rulandské bílé,** a semidry Burgundy-like white, has a flowery bouquet and full-bodied flavor. It's a good complement to poultry and veal. The dry, smooth flavor of **Ryzlink Rýnský** (the Rhine Riesling grape) is best enjoyed with cold entrées and fish. **Veltlínské zelené,** distinguished by its beautiful light-green color, also goes well with cold entrées.

Belying the notion that northerly climes are more auspicious for white than red grapes, northern Bohemia's scant few hundred acres of vineyards produce reliable reds and the occasional jewel. The leading wineries are found in the towns of Roudnice and Mělník, near the confluence of the Vltava and Labe (Elbe) rivers. **Frankovka,** fiery red and slightly acidic, is well suited to game and grilled meats. **Rulandské červené,** cherry-red in color and flavor, makes an excellent dry companion to poultry and game. **Vavřinecké,** the country's favorite red, dark and slightly sweet, also stands up well to red meats.

When to Tour

Prague is beautiful year-round, but avoid midsummer (especially July and August) and the Christmas and Easter holidays, when the city is overrun with tourists. Spring and fall generally combine good weather with a more bearable level of tourism. During the winter months you'll encounter few other visitors and have the opportunity to see Prague breathtakingly covered in snow; but it can get very cold. Bear in mind that many castles and museums are closed November through March.

The Czech government publishes an annual "Calendar of Tourist Events" in English, available from Čedok or the Prague Information Service. Čedok offices can provide you with exact dates and additional information.

In March, there is the **Prague City of Music Festival**; in May, the **Prague Spring Music Festival** (✉ Hellichova 18, 118 00 Prague 1, ☎ 02/533473); the **Prague Marathon**; and the **Prague Writers' Festival** (Viola Theater, ✉ Národní 7, Prague 1, ☎ 02/2422–0844) which offers dramatic readings by major writers from around the world.

In June, there is the **Prague International Film Festival**; in July, the **Prague Summer Culture Festival**; in September, the **Prague Autumn International Music Festival** (✉ Sekaninova 26, 120 00 Prague 2, ☎ 02/692–7470); the **AghaRTA International Jazz Festival** is in October, as well as the **Festival of 20th Century Music** (✉ Festa Arts Agency, Dlouhá 10, 110 00 Prague 1, ☎ 02/232–1086).

2 Exploring Prague

By Mark Baker

Updated by Ky Krauthamer and Martha Lagace

THE SPINE OF THE CITY is the river Vltava (also known as the Moldau), which runs through the city from south to north with a single sharp curve to the east. Prague originally comprised five independent towns, represented today by its main historic districts: **Hradčany** (Castle Area), **Malá Strana** (Lesser Quarter), **Staré Město** (Old Town), **Nové Město** (New Town), and **Josefov** (the Jewish Quarter).

Hradčany, the seat of Czech royalty for hundreds of years, has as its center the **Pražský Hrad** (Prague Castle), which overlooks the city from its hilltop west of the Vltava. Steps lead down from Hradčany to Malá Strana, an area dense with ornate mansions built by 17th- and 18th-century nobility.

Karlův Most (Charles Bridge) connects Malá Strana with Staré Město. Just a few blocks east of the bridge is the focal point of the Old Town, **Staroměstské náměstí** (Old Town Square). Staré Město is bounded by the curving Vltava and three large commercial avenues: **Revoluční** to the east, **Na příkopě** to the southeast, and **Národní třída** to the south.

Beyond lies the Nové Město; several blocks south is **Karlovo náměstí,** the city's largest square. Roughly 1 kilometer (½ mile) farther south is **Vyšehrad,** an ancient castle site high above the river.

On a promontory to the east of Wenceslas Square stretches **Vinohrady,** once the favored neighborhood of well-to-do Czechs; below Vinohrady lie the crumbling neighborhoods of **Žižkov** to the north and **Nusle** to the south. On the west bank of the Vltava south and east of Hradčany lie many older residential neighborhoods and enormous parks. About 3 kilometers (2 miles) from the center in every direction, Communist-era housing projects begin their unsightly sprawl.

THE OLD TOWN

A Good Walk

Numbers in the text correspond to numbers in the margin and on the Exploring Prague map.

Václavské náměstí (Wenceslas Square) ①, marked by the **Statue of St. Wenceslas** ② and convenient to hotels and transportation, is an excellent place to begin a tour of the Old Town (Staré Město). A long, gently sloping boulevard rather than a square in the usual sense, Václavské náměstí is bounded at the top (the southern end) by the **Národní Muzeum** (Czech National Museum) ③ and at the bottom by the pedestrian shopping areas of **Národní třída** and **Na příkopě**. Today Wenceslas Square comprises Prague's liveliest street scene. Don't miss the dense maze of arcades tucked away from the street in buildings that line both sides. You'll find an odd assortment of cafés, discos, ice-cream parlors, and movie houses, all seemingly unfazed by the passage of time. At night the square changes character somewhat as dance music pours out from the crowded discos and leather-jacketed cronies crowd around the taxi stands. One eye-catching building on the square is the **Hotel Europa** ④, at No. 25, a riot of art nouveau that recalls the glamorous world of turn-of-the-century Prague. To begin the approach to the Old Town proper, walk past the tall, art deco Koruna complex and turn right onto the handsome pedestrian zone called **Na příkopě**. Turn left onto Havířská ulice and follow this small alley to the glittering green-and-cream splendor of the renovated **Stavovské Divadlo** (Estates Theater) ⑤.

Return to Na příkopě, turn left, and continue to the end of the street. On weekdays between 8 AM and 5 PM, it's well worth taking a peek at the stunning interior of the **Živnostenská banka** (Merchants' Bank) ⑥, at No. 20.

Na příkopě ends abruptly at the **Náměstí Republiky** (Republic Square) ⑦, an important New Town transportation hub (with a metro stop). The severe Depression-era facade of the **Česka Národní banka** (Czech National Bank, Na příkopě 30) makes the building look more like a fortress than the nation's central bank. Close by stands the stately **Prašná brána** (Powder Tower), its festive Gothic spires looming above the square. Adjacent to the dignified Powder Tower, the

Exploring Prague

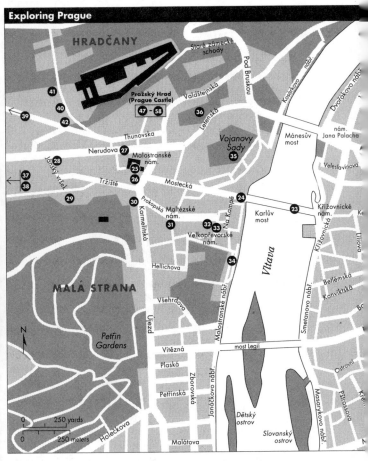

Betlémská kaple, **17**	Karlův most (Charles Bridge), **23**	Loreto Church, **39**
Bretfeld Palác, **28**	Kostel sv. Jiljí, **16**	Maiselova synagóga, **22**
Chrám Sv. Mikuláše, **26**	Kostel sv. Martina ve zdi, **18**	Malá Strana Bridge Towers, **24**
Clam-Gallas Palota, **15**	Kostel sv. Mikuláše, **13**	Malé náměstí, **14**
Hotel Europa, **4**	Kostel Nejsvětějšího, **45**	Malostranské náměstí, **25**
Hradčanské náměstí, **40**	Lennon Peace Wall, **33**	Maltézské náměstí, **31**
Jan Hus Monument, **11**	Letenské Sady, **43**	Náměstí Republiky, **7**
Kampa Island, **34**		

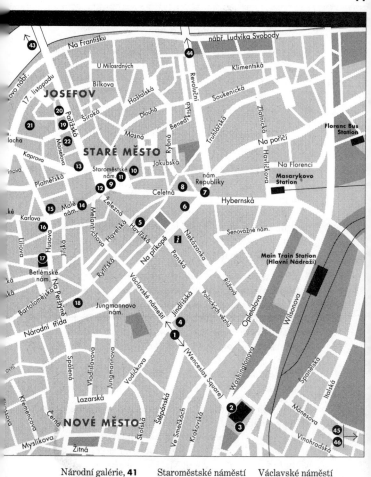

Národní galérie, **41**
Národní muzeum, **3**
Nerudova ulice, **27**
Pohořelec, **37**
Schönbornský palác, **29**
Schwarzenberský palác, **42**
Sixt House, **8**
Staroměstská radnice, **12**

Staroměstské náměstí (Old Town Square), **9**
Staronová synagóga, **20**
Starý židovský hřbitov, **21**
Statue of St. Wenceslas, **2**
Stavovské divadlo, **5**
Strahovský klášter, **38**
Týn Church, **10**

Václavské náměstí (Wenceslas Square), **1**
Veletržní palác, **44**
Velkopřevorské náměstí, **32**
Vojanovy Sady, **35**
Vrtbovský palác, **30**
Vysoká synagóga, **19**
Zahrada Valdštejnského paláca, **36**
Živnoské hřbitovy, **46**
Živnostenská banka, **6**

Obecní dům (Municipal House), under reconstruction until 1997, is a showcase for the art nouveau movement.

Walk through the arch at the base of the Powder Tower and down the formal **Celetná ulice** ⑧, the first leg of the so-called Royal Way. Monarchs favored this route primarily for its stunning entry into **Staroměstské náměstí** (Old Town Square) and because the houses along Celetná were among the city's finest, providing a suitable backdrop to the coronation procession. The pink Sixt House, at Celetná 2, sports one of the street's handsomest, if restrained, baroque facades.

Staroměstské náměstí (Old Town Square) ⑨, at the end of Celetná, is dazzling, thanks partly to the double-spired **Týn Church** (Kostel Panny Marie před Týnem) ⑩, which rises over the square from behind a row of patrician houses. To the immediate left of Týn Church is **U Zvonů** (No. 13), a baroque structure that has been stripped down to its original Gothic elements.

A short walk away stands the gorgeous pink-and-ocher **Palác Kinských** (Kinský Palace). At this end of the square, you can't help noticing the expressive **Jan Hus monument** ⑪. Opposite the Týn Church is the Gothic **Staroměstská radnice** (Old Town Hall) ⑫, which with its impressive 200-foot tower, gives the square its sense of importance. As the hour approaches, join the crowds milling below the tower's 15th-century **astronomical clock** for a brief but eerie spectacle taken straight from the Middle Ages, every hour on the hour.

Walk north along the edge of the small park beside Town Hall to reach the baroque **Kostel svatého Mikuláše** (Church of St. Nicholas) ⑬, not to be confused with the Lesser Town's St. Nicholas Church, on the other side of the river (☞ A Good Walk *in* Charles Bridge and Malá Strana, *below*).

Franz Kafka's birthplace is just to the left of St. Nicholas on U radnice. A small plaque can be found on the side of the house. Continue southwest from Old Town Square until you come to **Malé náměstí** (Small Square) ⑭, a nearly perfect ensemble of facades dating from the Middle Ages. Look for tiny **Karlova ulice,** which begins in the southwest corner of Malé náměstí, and take another quick right to stay on it (watch the signs—this medieval street seems designed to confound the visitor). Turn left at the T intersection

The Old Town

where Karlova seems to end in front of the Středočeská Galérie and continue left down the quieter Husova Street. Pause and inspect the exotic **Clam-Gallas palota** (Clam-Gallas Palace) ⑮, at Husova 20. You'll recognize it easily: Look for the Titans in the doorway holding up what must be a very heavy baroque facade.

Return to the T and continue down Husova. For a glimpse of a less successful baroque reconstruction, take a close look at the **Kostel svatého Jiljí** (Church of St. Giles) ⑯, across from No. 7.

Continue walking along Husova třída to Na Perštýně and turn right at tiny Betlémská ulice. The alley opens up onto a quiet square of the same name (Betlémská náměstí) and upon the most revered of all Hussite churches in Prague, the **Betlémská kaple** (Bethlehem Chapel) ⑰.

Return to Na Perštýně and continue walking to the right. As you near the back of the buildings of the busy **Národní třída** (National Boulevard), turn left at Martinská ulice. At the end of the street, the forlorn but majestic church **Kostel svatého Martina ve zdi** (St. Martin-in-the-Wall) ⑱ stands like a postwar ruin. Walk around the church to the left and through a little archway of apartments onto the bustling Národní třída. To the left, a five-minute walk away, lies Wenceslas Square and the starting point of the walk.

TIMING

Now that Prague is such a popular travel destination, the Wenceslas Square and Old Town Square areas are busy with activity around-the-clock almost all year round. Visitors in search of a little peace and quiet will find the streets at their most subdued on early weekend summer mornings or right after a sudden downpour; otherwise, expect to share Prague's pleasures. The streets in this walking tour are reasonably close together and can be covered in half a day, or in a full day if you have more time.

Sights To See

⑰ **Betlémská kaple** (Bethlehem Chapel). The church's elegant simplicity is in stark contrast to the diverting Gothic and baroque of the rest of the city. The original structure dates from the end of the 14th century, and Jan Hus himself was a regular preacher here from 1402 until his death in 1415. After the Thirty Years' War the church fell into the hands of the Jesuits and was finally demolished in 1786. Excavations carried out after World War I uncovered the original portal and three windows, and the entire church was reconstructed during the 1950s. Although little remains of the first church, some remnants of Hus's teachings can still be read on the inside walls. ⊠ *Betlémské nám. 5.* 🎟 *Admission charged.* ☉ *Apr.–Sept., daily 9–6; Oct.–Mar., daily 9–5.*

❽ Celetná ulice (Celetna Street). Most of the facades indicate the buildings are from the 17th or 18th century, but appearances are deceiving: Many of the houses in fact have foundations dating from the 12th century or earlier. **Sixt House,** at Celetná 2, dates from the 12th century—its Romanesque vaults are still visible in the wine restaurant in the basement.

❶❺ Clam-Gallas palota (Clam-Gallas Palace). The palace dates from 1713 and is the work of Johann Bernhard Fischer von Erlach, the famed Viennese architectural virtuoso of the day. Enter the building (push past the guard as if you know what you're doing) for a glimpse of the finely carved staircase, the work of the master himself, and of the Italian frescoes featuring Apollo that surround it. The Gallas family was prominent during the 18th century but has long since died out. The building now houses the municipal archives and is rarely open to visitors. ⊠ *Husova 20.*

Franz Kafka's birthplace. For years this memorial to Kafka's birth (July 3, 1883) was the only public acknowledgment of the writer's stature in world literature, reflecting the traditionally ambiguous attitude of the Czech government to his work. The Communists were always too uncomfortable with Kafka's themes of bureaucracy and alienation to sing his praises too loudly, if at all. As a German and a Jew, moreover, Kafka could easily be dismissed as standing outside the mainstream of Czech literature. Following the 1989 revolution, however, Kafka's popularity soared, and his works are now widely available in Czech. A fascinating little museum has been set up in the house of his birth. ⊠ *U radnice 5.* 🎟 *20 Kč.* ☉ *Tues.–Sat. 10–6 (until 7 in summer).*

The Old Town

④ Hotel Europa. An art-nouveau gem, it has elegant stained glass and mosaics in the café and restaurant. The terrace, serving drinks in the summer, is an excellent spot for people-watching. ✉ *Václavské nám. 25.*

⑪ Jan Hus monument. Few memorials have elicited as much controversy as this one, which was dedicated in July 1915, exactly 500 years after Hus was burned at the stake in Constance, Germany. Some maintain that the monument's Secessionist style (the inscription seems to come right from turn-of-the-century Vienna) clashes with the Gothic and baroque of the square. Others dispute the romantic depiction of Hus, who appears here in flowing garb as tall and bearded. The real Hus, historians maintain, was short and had a baby face. Still, no one can take issue with the influence of this fiery preacher, whose ability to transform doctrinal disputes, both literally and metaphorically, into the language of the common man made him into a religious and national symbol for the Czechs. ✉ *Staroměstské nám.*

Karlova ulice. The character of Karlova ulice has changed in recent years to meet the growing number of tourists. Galleries and gift shops now occupy almost every storefront. But the cobblestones, narrow alleys, and crumbling gables still make it easy to imagine what life was like 400 years ago.

⑯ Kostel svatého Jiljí (Church of St. Giles). This baroque church was another important outpost of Czech Protestantism in the 16th century. The exterior is a powerful example of Gothic architecture, including the buttresses and a characteristic portal; the interior, surprisingly, is baroque, dating from the 17th century. ✉ *Across from Husova 7.*

⑱ Kostel svatého Martina ve zdi (St. Martin-in-the-Wall). It was here in 1414 that Holy Communion was first given to the Bohemian laity—with both bread and wine, in defiance of the Catholic custom of the time, which dictated that only bread was to be offered to the masses, with wine reserved for the priests and clergy. From then on, the chalice came to symbolize the Hussite movement.

⑬ Kostel svatého Mikuláše (Church of St. Nicholas). Designed in the 18th century by Prague's own master of late baroque, Kilian Ignaz Dientzenhofer, this church is probably less successful than its namesake across town in capturing the style's lyric exuberance. Still, Dientzenhofer utilized the limited space to create a structure that neither dominates nor retreats from the imposing square. The interior is compact, with a beautiful but small chandelier and an enormous black organ that seems to overwhelm the rear of the church. The church often hosts afternoon and evening concerts.

⓮ Malé náměstí (Small Square). Note the Renaissance iron fountain dating from 1560 in the center of the square. The sgraffito on the house at No. 3 is not as old (1890) as it looks, but here and there you can find authentic Gothic portals and Renaissance sgraffiti that betray the square's true age.

Na příkopě. The name means "at the moat," harking back to the time when the street was indeed a moat separating the Old Town on the left from the New Town on the right. Today the pedestrian zone Na příkopě is prime shopping territory, its smaller boutiques considered far more elegant than the motley collection of stores on Wenceslas Square. But don't expect much real elegance here: After 40 years of Communist orthodoxy in the fashion world, it will be many years before the boutiques really can match Western European standards.

❼ Náměstí Republiky (Republic Square). Although an important New Town transportation hub (with a metro stop), the square has never really come together as a vital public space, perhaps because of its jarring architectural eclecticism. Taken one by one, each building is interesting in its own right, but the ensemble is less than the sum of the parts.

❸ Národní Muzeum (Czech National Museum). This imposing structure, designed by Prague architect Josef Schulz and built between 1885 and 1890, does not come into its own until it is bathed in nighttime lighting. By day the grandiose edifice seems an inappropriate venue for a musty collection of stones and bones, minerals, and coins. This museum is only for dedicated fans of the genre. ✉ *Václavské nám. 68,* ☎ *02/2423–0485.* 🖃 *40 Kč.* ☉ *Daily 9–5; closed 1st Tues. of month.*

Obecní dům (Municipal House). When reconstruction ends, this building should return to its former glory as a center for

The Old Town

concerts and fashionable restaurants. The style, mature art nouveau, recalls the lengths the Czech middle classes went to at the turn of the century to imitate Paris, then the epitome of style and glamour. Much of the interior bears the work of the art-nouveau master Alfons Mucha and other leading Czech artists. Mucha decorated the main Hall of the Lord Mayor upstairs, with impressive, magical frescoes depicting Czech history. The beautiful Smetana Hall is on the second floor. Guided tours are available. ✉ *Nám. Republiky 5.*

> **NEED A BREAK?** If you prefer subtle elegance, head around the corner to the café at **Hotel Paříž** (✉ U Obecního domu 1, ☎ 2422–2151), a Jugendstil jewel tucked away on a relatively quiet street.

Palác Kinských (Kinský Palace). Built in 1765, this is considered one of Prague's finest late-baroque structures. With its exaggerated pink overlay and numerous statues, the facade looks extreme when contrasted with the more staid baroque elements of other nearby buildings. The palace once housed a German school (where Franz Kafka was a student for nine misery-laden years) and presently contains the National Gallery's graphics collection. The main exhibition room is on the second floor; exhibits change every few months and are usually worth seeing. It was from this building that Communist leader Klement Gottwald, flanked by his comrade Clementis, first addressed the crowds after seizing power in February 1948—an event recounted in the first chapter of Milan Kundera's novel *The Book of Laughter and Forgetting*. ✉ *Staroměstské nám. 12.* 🎫 *20 Kč.* ⊙ *Tues.–Sun. 10–6.*

Prašná brána (Powder Tower). Construction of the tower, one of the city's 13 original gates, was begun by King Vladislav II of Jagiello in 1475. At the time, the kings of Bohemia maintained their royal residence next door (on the site of the current Obecní dům, the Municipal House), and the tower was intended to be the grandest gate of all. But Vladislav was Polish and thus heartily disliked by the rebellious Czech citizens of Prague. Nine years after he assumed power, fearing for his life, he moved the royal court across the river to Prague Castle. Work on the tower was abandoned, and the half-finished structure was used for storing gunpowder—hence its odd name—until the end of the 17th century. The oldest part of the tower is the base; the golden spires were not added until the end of the last century. The climb to the top affords a striking view of the Old Town and Prague Castle in the distance. ⊠ *Nám. Republiky.* ☎ *20 Kč.* ☉ *Apr.–Oct., daily 9–6.*

★ ⑨ **Staroměstské náměstí** (Old Town Square). Dazzling. Long the heart of the Old Town, the square grew to its present proportions when the city's original marketplace was moved away from the river in the 12th century. Its shape and appearance have changed little over the years. During the day the square has a festive atmosphere as musicians vie for the favor of onlookers, hefty young men in medieval outfits mint coins, and artists display renditions of Prague street scenes. If you come back to the square at night, the crowds thin out, and the unlit shadowy towers of the Týn Church (to your right as you enter the square) rise ominously over the glowing baroque facades.

In 1422 the radical Czech Hussite preacher Jan Želivský was executed here for his part in storming the New Town's town hall. Three Catholic consuls and seven German citizens were thrown out of the window in the ensuing fray— the first of Prague's many famous defenestrations. Within a few years, the Hussites had taken over the town, expelled the Germans, and set up their own administration.

⑫ **Staroměstská radnice** (Old Town Hall). As you walk toward the building from the Jan Hus monument (☞ *above*), look for the 27 white crosses on the ground just in front of the Town Hall. These mark the spot where 27 Bohemian noblemen were killed by the Hapsburgs in 1621 during the dark days following the defeat of the Czechs at the Battle of White Mountain. The grotesque spectacle, designed to quash any further national or religious opposition, took some five hours to complete, as the men were put to the sword or hanged one by one.

The Town Hall has served as the center of administration for the Old Town since 1338, when King Johann of Luxembourg first granted the city council the right to a permanent location. Walk around the structure to the left and you'll see it's actually a series of houses jutting into the square; they

The Old Town

were purchased over the years and successively added to the complex. The most interesting is the **U Minuty**, the corner building to the left of the clock tower, with its 16th-century Renaissance sgraffiti of biblical and classical motifs.

The impressive 200-foot **Town Hall Tower** was first built in the 14th century and given its current late-Gothic appearance around 1500 by the master Matyáš Rejsek. For a rare view of the Old Town and its maze of crooked streets and alleyways, climb to the top of the tower. The climb is not strenuous, but steep stairs at the top unfortunately prevent people with disabilities from enjoying the view. Enter through the door to the left of the tower.

Just before the hour, look to the upper part of the **astronomical clock,** where a skeleton begins by tolling a death knell and turning an hour-glass upside down. The Twelve Apostles parade momentarily, and then a cockerel flaps its wings and crows, piercing the air as the hour finally strikes, solemnly. To the right of the skeleton, the dreaded Turk nods his head, seemingly hinting at another invasion like those of the 16th and 17th centuries. Immediately after the hour, guided tours in English and German (German only in winter) of the Town Hall depart from the main desk inside. However, the only notable features inside are the fine Renaissance ceilings and the Gothic Council Room. ⊠ *Staroměstské nám.* ☜ *To all sights 20 Kč.* ⊙ *Daily 9–6 (until 5 in winter).*

NEED A BREAK? Staroměstské náměstí is a convenient spot for refreshments. **Tchibo,** at No. 6 (☎ 2481–1026), has tasty sandwiches and pastries, excellent coffee, and an outdoor terrace in season.

---

❷ **Statue of St. Wenceslas.** In 1848 citizens protested Hapsburg rule at this statue in front of the National Museum. In 1939 residents gathered to oppose Hitler's takeover of Bohemia and Moravia. It was here also, in 1969, that the student Jan Palach set himself on fire to protest the bloody invasion of his country by the Soviet Union and other Warsaw Pact countries in August of the previous year. The invasion ended the "Prague Spring," a cultural and political movement emphasizing free expression, which was supported by Alexander Dubček, the popular leader at the time.

Although Dubček never intended to dismantle Communist authority completely, his political and economic reforms proved too daring for fellow comrades in the rest of Eastern Europe. In the months following the invasion, conservatives loyal to the Soviet Union were installed in all influential positions. The subsequent two decades were a period of cultural stagnation. Thousands of residents left the country or went underground; many more resigned themselves to lives of minimal expectations and small pleasures. ⊠ *Václavské nám.*

❺ Stavovské Divadlo (Estates Theater). Built in the 1780s in the classical style and reopened in 1991 after years of renovation, the handsome theater was for many years a beacon of Czech-language culture in a city long dominated by the German variety. It is probably best known as the site of the world premiere of Mozart's opera *Don Giovanni* in October 1787, with the composer himself conducting. Prague audiences were quick to acknowledge Mozart's genius: The opera was an instant hit here, though it flopped nearly everywhere else in Europe. Mozart wrote most of the opera's second act in Prague at the Villa Bertramka, where he was a frequent guest. ⊠ *Ovocný trh.*

★ **❿ Týn Church** (Kostel Panny Marie před Týnem). Construction of its twin jet-black spires, which still jar the eye, was begun by King Jiří of Poděbrad in 1461, during the heyday of the Hussites. Jiří had a gilded chalice, the symbol of the Hussites, proudly displayed on the front gable between the two towers. Following the defeat of the Hussites by the Catholic Hapsburgs, the chalice was removed and eventually replaced by a Madonna. As a final blow, the chalice was melted down and made into the Madonna's glimmering halo (you still can see it by walking into the center of the square and looking up between the spires). The entrance to Týn Church is through the arcades, under the house at No. 604.

Although the exterior of Týn Church is one of the best examples of Prague Gothic (in part the work of Peter Parler, architect of the Charles Bridge and St. Vitus Cathedral), much of the interior, including the tall nave, was rebuilt in the baroque style in the 17th century. Some Gothic pieces remain, however: Look to the left of the main altar for a beautifully preserved set of early Gothic carvings. The main altar itself was painted by Karel Şkréta, a luminary of the Czech Baroque. Before leaving the church, look for the grave marker (tucked away to the right of the main altar) of the great Danish astronomer Tycho Brahe, who came to Prague as "Imperial Mathematicus" in 1599 under Rudolf II. As a scientist, Tycho had a place in history that is assured: Johannes Kepler (another resident of the Prague court) used Tycho's observations to formulate his laws of planetary motion. But it is myth that has endeared Tycho to the hearts of Prague residents: The robust Dane, who was apparently fond of duels, lost part of his nose in one (take a closer look at the marker). He quickly had a wax nose fashioned for everyday use but preferred to parade around on holidays and festive occasions sporting a bright silver one. ✉ *Celetná 5.*

U Zvonů. This baroque-cum-Gothic structure occasionally hosts concerts and art exhibitions. The exhibitions change frequently, and it's worth stopping by to see what's on. ✉ *Celetná 13.*

❶ **Václavské náměstí** (Wenceslas Square). Visitors may recognize this spot from their television sets, for it was here that some 500,000 students and citizens gathered in the heady days of November 1989 to protest the policies of the former Communist regime. The government capitulated after a week of demonstrations, without a shot fired or the loss of a single life, bringing to power the first democratic government in 40 years (under playwright-president Václav Havel). Today this peaceful transfer of power is proudly referred to as the "Velvet" or "Gentle" Revolution (*něžná revolucia*). It was only fitting that the 1989 revolution should take place on Wenceslas Square. Throughout much of Czech history, the square has served as the focal point for popular discontent. Although Wenceslas Square was first laid out by Charles IV in 1348 as the center of the New Town (Nové Město), few buildings of architectural merit line the square today.

❻ **Živnostenská banka** (Merchants' Bank). The style, a tasteful example of 19th-century exuberance, reflected the city's growing prosperity at the time. Ignore the guards and walk up the decorated stairs to the beautiful main banking room (note, however, that taking photos is forbidden). ✉ *Na příkopě 20.*

THE JEWISH GHETTO

Prague's Jews survived centuries of discrimination, but two unrelated events of modern times have left their historic ghetto little more than a collection of museums. Around 1900, city officials decided for hygienic purposes to raze the ghetto and pave over its crooked streets. Only the synagogues, the town hall, and a few other buildings survived this early attempt at urban renewal. The second event was the Holocaust. Under Nazi occupation, a staggering percentage of the city's Jews were deported and murdered in concentration camps. Of the 35,000 Jews living in the ghetto before World War II, only about 1,200 returned to resettle the neighborhood after the war.

A Good Walk

Numbers in the text correspond to numbers in the margin and on the Exploring Prague map.

To reach **Josefov**, the Jewish ghetto, leave Staroměstské náměsti (Old Town Square) via the handsome Pařížská and head north toward the river and the Hotel Inter-Continental. The festive atmosphere changes suddenly as you enter the area of the ghetto. The buildings are lower here, and older; the mood is hushed. Treasures and artifacts of the ghetto are now the property of the **Státní židovské muzeum** (State Jewish Museum), a complex comprising the Old Jewish Cemetery and the collections of the remaining individual synagogues. On Červená ulice is the **Vysoká synagóga** (High Synagogue) ⑲; adjacent, at Maislova 18, is the **Židovská radnice** (Jewish Town Hall), now home to the Jewish Community Center. The **Staronová synagóga** (Old-New Synagogue) ⑳ across the street at Červená 2 is the oldest standing synagogue in Europe.

Continue along Červená ulice, which becomes the little street **U starého hřbitova** (At the Old Cemetery) beyond Maislova ulice. At the bend in the road lies the Jewish ghetto's most astonishing sight, the **Starý židovský hřbitov** (Old Jewish

The Jewish Ghetto

Cemetery) ㉑. Just to the right of the cemetery entrance is the **Obřadní síň** (Ceremony Hall), which houses a moving exhibition of drawings made by children held at the Nazi concentration camp at Terezín (Theresienstadt), in northern Bohemia. If you were to continue in the other direction through the cemetery, you would come to the **Pinkasova synagóga** (Pinkas Synagogue), a handsome Gothic structure. Return to Maislova ulice via U starého hřbitova and turn right in the direction of the Old Town once again, crossing Široká ulice. Look in at the enormous collection of silver articles of worship in the **Maislova synagóga** (Maisel Synagogue) ㉒.

TIMING

The Jewish ghetto is one of the most popular visitor destinations in Prague, especially in the height of summer, when its tiny streets are jammed to bursting with tourists almost all the time. The best time to savor any of these sights without any crowds and distractions would be early morning when the museums and cemetery first open. The area itself is very compact and a basic walk-through should take only half a day. Travelers who'd like to linger in the museums could easily spend two days or more exploring this area.

Sights to See

㉒ **Maislova synagóga** (Maisel Synagogue). This houses a huge number of silver articles of worship confiscated by the Nazis from synagogues throughout Central Europe. Here you'll find the State Jewish Museum's finest collection of Torah wrappers and mantles, silver pointers, breastplates, spice boxes, candleholders (the eight-branched *Hanukkiah* and the seven-branched menorah), and Levite washing sets. ⊠ *Maislova 10.* 🕾 *For admission information to this and other synagogues, see entry under Státní židovské muzeum.*

Obřadní síň (Ceremony Hall). It now houses drawings made by children at the Nazi concentration camp Terezín. During the early years of the war the Nazis used the camp for propaganda purposes to demonstrate their "humanity" toward the Jews, and prisoners were given relative freedom to lead "normal" lives. Transports to death camps in Poland began in earnest in the final months of the war, however, and many thousands of Terezín prisoners, including many of these children, eventually perished. 🕾 *For admission information to the hall, see entry under Státní židovské muzeum.*

Pařížská Street. The buildings on this street date from the end of the 19th century, and their elegant facades reflect the prosperity of the Czech middle classes at the time. Here and there you can spot the influence of the Viennese Jugendstil, with its emphasis on mosaics, geometric forms, and gold inlay. The look is fresh against the busier 19th-century revival facades of most of the other structures.

Pinkasova synagóga (Pinkas Synagogue). Further testimony to the appalling crimes perpetrated against the Jews during World War II can be seen in this newly renovated synagogue. The names of 77,297 Bohemian and Moravian Jews murdered by the Nazis were inscribed in rows on the walls inside (many of the names, sadly, have been destroyed by water damage). The building's foundation dates from the 11th century. Enter the synagogue from Široká Street on the other side of the cemetery, or through the cemetery. *For admission information to this and other synagogues, see entry under Státní židovské muzeum.*

㉠ Staronová synagóga (Old-New Synagogue). Dating from the mid-13th century, it is one of the most important works of early Gothic in Prague. The odd name recalls the legend that the synagogue was built on the site of an ancient Jewish temple and that stones from the temple were used to build the present structure. The synagogue has not only survived fires and the razing of the ghetto at the end of the last century but also emerged from the Nazi occupation intact; it is still in active use. The oldest part of the synagogue is the entrance, with its vault supported by two pillars. The grille at the center of the hall dates from the 15th century. Note that men are required to cover their heads inside and that during services men and women sit apart. ✉ Červená 2.

★ **㉑ Starý židovský hřbitov** (Old Jewish Cemetery). An unforgettable sight, this melancholy space not far from the busy city was, from the 14th century to 1787, the final resting place for all Jews living in Prague. Some 12,000 graves in all are piled atop one another in 12 layers. Walk the paths amid the gravestones. The relief symbols represent the name or profession of the deceased. The oldest marked grave belongs to the poet Avigdor Kara, who died in 1439. The best-known marker is probably that of Jehuda ben Beza-

The Jewish Ghetto

lel, the famed Rabbi Loew, who is credited with having created the mythical Golem in 1573. Even today, small scraps of paper bearing wishes are stuffed into the cracks of the rabbi's tomb in the hope he will grant them. Loew's grave lies just a few steps from the entrance, near the western wall of the cemetery.

Státní židovské muzeum (State Jewish Museum). All the synagogues and the Old Jewish Cemetery are under the auspices of this museum. In a bit of irony, the holdings are vast thanks to Hitler, who had planned to open a museum here documenting the life and practices of what he had hoped would be an "extinct" people. The cemetery and most of the synagogues are open to the public. Each synagogue specializes in certain artifacts, and you can buy tickets for all the buildings at either Maislova synagóga, Pinkasova synagóga, Vysoká synagóga, or in front of the Old Jewish Cemetery. ☎ 02/231–0681. *Combined ticket to Jewish Museum collections and Old Jewish Cemetery 270 Kč; museum collections only, 150 Kč; Old Jewish Cemetery only, 120 Kč.* ☉ *Apr.–May, Sun.–Fri. 9–6; June–Oct., Sun.–Fri. 9–6:30; Nov.–Mar., Sun.–Fri. 9–4:30; closed Jewish holidays.*

⑲ Vysoká synagóga (High Synagogue). This striking building features rich Torah mantles and silver. It was ordered built in the second half of the 16th century by the banker and businessman Mordecai Maisel (☞ Jewish Town Hall, *below*) and was expanded at the end of the 17th century. ✉ *Červená ul. (enter at No. 101).* *For admission information to this and other synagogues, see entry under Státní židovské muzeum.*

★ Židovská radnice (Jewish Town Hall). The hall was the creation of Mordecai Maisel, an influential Jewish leader at the end of the 16th century. It was restored in the 18th century and given its clock and bell tower at that time. A second clock, with Hebrew numbers, keeps time counterclockwise. Now home to the Jewish Community Center, the building also houses Prague's only kosher restaurant, Shalom. ✉ *Maislova 18.*

CHARLES BRIDGE AND MALÁ STRANA

Karlův most (the Charles Bridge), a beautiful gothic bridge embellished with baroque statues, connects the Old Town with one of Prague's most exquisite neighborhoods, Malá Strana (the so-called Lesser Quarter, or Little Town). Malá Strana was established in 1257 and for years was home to the merchants and craftsmen who served the royal court.

A Good Walk

Numbers in the text correspond to numbers in the margin and on the Exploring Prague map.

Prague's **Malá Strana** is not for the methodical traveler. Its charm lies in the tiny lanes, the sudden blasts of bombastic architecture, and the soul-stirring views that emerge for a second before disappearing behind the sloping roofs.

Begin the tour on the Old Town side of **Karlův most** (Charles Bridge) ㉓, which you can reach by foot in about 10 minutes from the Old Town Square. Rising above it is the majestic **Old Town Bridge Tower**; the climb of 138 steps is worth the effort for the views it affords of the Old Town and, across the river, of Malá Strana and Prague Castle.

It's worth pausing to take a closer look at some of the statues as you walk across Charles Bridge toward Malá Strana. Approaching Malá Strana, you'll see the Kampa Island below you, separated from the Lesser Town by an arm of the Vltava known as Čertovka (Devil's Stream).

By now you are almost at the end of the bridge. In front of you is the striking conjunction of the two **Malá Strana bridge towers** ㉔, one Gothic, the other Romanesque. Together they frame the baroque flamboyance of St. Nicholas Church in the distance. At night this is an absolutely wondrous sight. If you didn't climb the tower on the Old Town side of the bridge, it's worth scrambling up the wooden stairs inside the Gothic tower **Mostecká věž** for the views over the roofs of the Malá Strana and of the Old Town across the river.

Walk under the gateway of the towers into the little uphill street called **Mostecká ulice.** You have now entered the **Malá Strana** (Lesser Quarter). Follow Mostecká ulice up

Charles Bridge and Malá Strana

to the rectangular **Malostranské náměstí** (Lesser Quarter Square) ㉕, now the district's traffic hub rather than its heart. On the left side of the square stands **Chrám svatého Mikuláše** (St. Nicholas Church) ㉖.

Nerudova ulice ㉗ runs up from the square toward Prague Castle. Lined with gorgeous houses (and in recent years an ever-larger number of places to spend money), it's sometimes burdened with the moniker "Prague's most beautiful street." A tiny passageway at No. 13, on the left-hand side as you go up, leads to **Tržiště ulice** and the **Schöbornský palác** ㉙, once Franz Kafka's home, now the Embassy of the United States. The street winds down to the quarter's noisy main street, **Karmelitská,** where the famous "Infant of Prague" resides in the **Kostel Panny Marie vítězné.** Tiny **Prokopská ulice** leads off of Karmelitská, past the former Church of St. Procopius, now converted, oddly, into an apartment block, and into **Maltézské náměstí** ㉛, a characteristically noble compound. Nearby, **Velkopřevorské náměstí** ㉜ boasts even grander palaces.

A tiny bridge at the cramped square's lower end takes you across the little backwater called Čertovka to **Kampa Island** ㉞ and its broad lawns, cafés, and river views. Winding your way underneath the Charles Bridge and along the street **U lužického semináře** brings you to a quiet walled garden, **Vojanovy sady** ㉟. Another, more formal garden, with an unbeatable view of Prague Castle looming above, the **Zahrada Valdštejnského paláca** ㊱ hides itself off busy Letenská ulice near the Malostranská metro station.

TIMING

The area is at its best in the evening, when the softer light hides the crumbling facades and brings you into a world of glimmering beauty. The basic walk described here could take as little as half a day; longer if you'd like to explore the area's lovely nooks and crannies.

Sights To See

㉘ **Bretfeld palác** (Bretfeld Palace). It's worth taking a quick look at this rococo house on the corner of Nerudova ulice and Jánský vršek. The relief of St. Nicholas on the facade is the work of Ignaz Platzer, but the building is valued more for its historical associations than for its architecture:

This is where Mozart, his lyricist partner Lorenzo da Ponte, and the aging but still infamous philanderer and music lover Casanova stayed at the time of the world premiere of *Don Giovanni* in 1787. The Malá Strana gained a new connection with Mozart when its streets were used to represent 18th-century Vienna in the filming of Miloš Forman's *Amadeus*. ⊠ *Nerudova 33.*

The archway at Nerudova 13, more or less opposite the Santini-designed **Kostel Panny Marie ustavičné pomoci u Kajetánů** (Church of Our Lady of Perpetual Help at the Theatines), hides one of the many winding passageways that give the Malá Strana its enchantingly ghostly character at night. Follow the dogleg curve downhill, past two restaurants, vine-covered walls, and some broken-down houses. The alleyway really comes into its own only in the dark, the dim lighting hiding the grime and highlighting the mystery.

★ ㉖ **Chrám svatého Mikuláše** (St. Nicholas Church). With its dynamic curves, this church is one of the purest and most ambitious examples of high baroque. The celebrated architect Christoph Dientzenhofer began the Jesuit church in 1704 on the site of one of the more active Hussite churches of 15th-century Prague. Work on the building was taken over by his son Kilian Ignaz Dientzenhofer, who built the dome and presbytery; Anselmo Lurago completed the whole in 1755 by adding the bell tower. The juxtaposition of the broad, full-bodied dome with the slender bell tower is one of the many striking architectural contrasts that mark the Prague skyline. Inside, the vast pink-and-green space is impossible to take in with a single glance; every corner bristles with movement, guiding the eye first to the dramatic statues, then to the hectic frescoes, and on to the shining faux-marble pillars. Many of the statues are the work of Ignaz Platzer; they constitute his last blaze of success. When the centralizing and secularizing reforms of Joseph II toward the end of the 18th century brought an end to the flamboyant baroque era, Platzer's workshop was forced to declare bankruptcy. ⊠ *Malostranské nám.* 🖻 *20 Kč.* ☉ *Daily 9–4 (until 5 or 6 in summer).*

㉞ **Kampa Island.** Prague's largest island is cut off from the "mainland" by the narrow Čertovka streamlet. The name

Charles Bridge and Malá Strana

Čertovka translates as Devil's Stream and reputedly refers to a cranky old lady who once lived on Maltese Square (given the river's present filthy state, however, the name is ironically appropriate). The unusually well-kept lawns of the **Kampa Gardens** that occupy much of the island are one of the few places in Prague where sitting on the grass is openly tolerated. If it's a warm day, spread out a blanket and bask for a while in the sunshine. The row of benches that line the river to the left is also a popular spot from which to contemplate the city. At night this stretch along the river is especially romantic.

★ ❷❸ **Karlův most** (Charles Bridge). The view from the foot of the bridge on the Old Town side is nothing short of breathtaking, encompassing the towers and domes of Malá Strana and the soaring spires of St. Vitus Cathedral to the northwest. This heavenly vision, one of the most beautiful in Europe, changes subtly in perspective as you walk across the bridge, attended by the host of baroque saints that decorate the bridge's peaceful Gothic stones. At night its drama is spellbinding: St. Vitus Cathedral lit in a ghostly green, the castle in monumental yellow, and the Church of St. Nicholas in a voluptuous pink, all viewed through the menacing silhouettes of the bowed statues and the Gothic towers. If you do nothing else in Prague, you must visit the Charles Bridge at night. During the day the pedestrian bridge buzzes with activity. Street musicians vie with artisans hawking jewelry, paintings, and glass for the hearts and wallets of the passing multitude. At night the crowds thin out a little, the musicians multiply, and the bridge becomes a long block party—nearly everyone brings a bottle.

When the Přemyslide princes set up residence in Prague in the 10th century, there was a ford across the Vltava at this point, a vital link along one of Europe's major trading routes. After several wooden bridges and the first stone bridge had washed away in floods, Charles IV appointed the 27-year-old German Peter Parler, the architect of St. Vitus Cathedral, to build a new structure in 1357. After 1620, following the defeat of Czech Protestants by Catholic Hapsburgs at the Battle of White Mountain, the bridge and its adornment became caught up in the Catholic-Hussite (Protestant) conflict. The many baroque statues that began to appear in the late 17th century, commissioned by Catholics, eventually came to symbolize the totality of the Austrian (hence Catholic) triumph. The Czech writer Milan Kundera sees the statues from this perspective: "The thousands of saints looking out from all sides, threatening you, following you, hypnotizing you, are the raging hordes of occupiers who invaded Bohemia three hundred and fifty years ago to tear the people's faith and language from their hearts."

The religious conflict is less obvious nowadays, leaving only the artistic tension between baroque and Gothic that gives the bridge its allure. It's worth pausing to take a closer look at some of the statues as you walk toward Malá Strana. The third on the right, a brass crucifix with Hebrew lettering in gold, was mounted on the location of a wooden cross destroyed in the battle with the Swedes (the golden lettering was reputedly financed by a Jew accused of defiling the cross). The eighth statue on the right, St. John of Nepomuk, is the oldest of all; it was designed by Johann Brokoff in 1683. On the left-hand side, sticking out from the bridge between the 9th and 10th statues (the latter has a wonderfully expressive vanquished Satan), stands a Roland statue. This knightly figure, bearing the coat of arms of the Old Town, was once a reminder that this part of the bridge belonged to the Old Town before Prague became a unified city in 1784.

In the eyes of most art historians, the most valuable statue is the 12th, on the left. Mathias Braun's statue of St. Luitgarde depicts the blind saint kissing Christ's wounds. The most compelling grouping, however, is the second from the end on the left, a work of Ferdinand Maximilien Brokov from 1714. Here the saints are incidental; the main attraction is the Turk, his face expressing extreme boredom while guarding Christians imprisoned in the cage at his side. When the statue was erected, just 29 years after the second Turkish invasion of Vienna, it scandalized the Prague public, who smeared the statue with mud.

Kostel Panny Marie vítězné (Church of Our Lady Victorious). Just down the street from the **Vrtbovský palác** (☞ *below*), this comfortably ramshackle church makes the unlikely home of one of Prague's best-known religious artifacts, the *Pražské Jezulátko* (Infant Jesus of Prague). Originally brought to Prague from Spain in the 16th cen-

Charles Bridge and Malá Strana

tury, this tiny porcelain doll (now bathed in neon lighting straight out of Las Vegas) is renowned worldwide for showering miracles on anyone willing to kneel before it and pray. Nuns from a nearby convent arrive at dawn each day to change the infant's clothes; pieces of the doll's extensive wardrobe have been sent by believers from around the world. ⊠ *Karmelitská 9a.* 🖃 *Free.*

㉝ Lennon Peace Wall. Amid the pompous display of baroque finery stands a peculiar monument to the passive rebellion of Czech youth against the strictures of the former Communist regime. Under the Communists, Western rock music was officially discouraged, and students adopted the former Beatle as a symbol of resistance. Paintings of John Lennon and lyrics from his songs in Czech and English began to appear on the wall sometime in the 1980s. Even today, long after the Communists have departed, new graffiti still turns up regularly. It's not clear how long the police or the owners of the wall will continue to tolerate the massive amount of writing (which has started to spread to other walls around the neighborhood), but the volume of writing suggests that the Lennon myth continues to endure.

㉔ Malá Strana bridge towers. The lower, Romanesque tower formed a part of the earlier wooden and stone bridges, and its present appearance stems from a renovation in 1591. The Gothic tower, **Mostecká věž**, was added to the bridge a few decades after its completion. ⊠ *Mostecká ul.* 🖃 *20 Kč.* ☉ *Apr.–Oct., daily 9–6.*

㉕ Malostranské náměstí (Lesser Quarter Square). The arcaded houses on the left, dating from the 16th and 17th centuries, exhibit a mix of baroque and Renaissance elements.

㉛ Maltézské náměstí (Maltese Square). Peaceful and grandiose, this square was named for the Knights of Malta. In the middle is a sculpture depicting John the Baptist. This work, by Ferdinand Brokov, was erected in 1715 to commemorate the end of a plague. The relief on the far side shows Salome engrossed in her dance of the seven veils while John is being decapitated. There are two intricately decorated palaces on this square: to the right the rococo Turba Palace, now the Japanese Embassy, and at the bottom the Nostitz Palace, the Dutch Embassy.

㉗ Nerudova ulice. This steep little street used to be the last leg of the Royal Way, walked by the king before his coronation, and it is still the best way to get to Prague Castle. It was named for the 19th-century Czech journalist and poet Jan Neruda (after whom Chilean poet Pablo Neruda renamed himself). Until Joseph II's administrative reforms in the late 18th century, house numbering was unknown in Prague. Each house bore a name, depicted on the facade, and these are particularly prominent on Nerudova ulice. House No. 6, **U červeného orla** (At the Red Eagle), proudly displays a faded painting of a red eagle. Number 12 is known as **U tří housliček** (At the Three Violins). In the early 18th century, three generations of the Edlinger violin-making family lived here. Joseph II's scheme numbered each house according to its position in Prague's separate "towns" (here Malá Strana) rather than according to its sequence on the street. The red plates record these original house numbers; the blue ones are the numbers used in addresses today—except, oddly enough, in some of the newer suburbs—while, to confuse the tourist, many architectural guides refer to the old, red number plates.

NEED A BREAK?

Nerudova ulice is filled with little restaurants and snack bars and offers something for everyone. **U zeleného čaje**, at No. 19, is a fragrant little tearoom, offering fruit and herbal teas as well as light salads and sweets. **U Kocoura** at No. 2 is a traditional pub that hasn't caved in to touristic niceties.

Two palaces break the unity of the burghers' houses on Nerudova ulice. Both were designed by the adventurous baroque architect Giovanni Santini, one of the Italian builders most in demand by wealthy nobles of the early 18th century. The **Morzin Palace,** on the left at No. 5, is now the Romanian Embassy. The fascinating facade, with an allegory of night and day, was created in 1713 and is the work of F. M. Brokov of Charles Bridge statue fame. Across the street at No. 20 is the **Thun-Hohenstein Palace,** now the Italian Embassy. The gateway with two enormous eagles (the emblem of the Kolovrat family, who owned the building at the time) is the work of the other great Charles Bridge statue sculptor, Mathias Braun. Santini himself lived at No. 14, the so-called **Valkoun House.**

In case you want to be welcomed there.

We're here to see that you're always welcomed at establishments everywhere. That's why millions of people carry the American Express® Card – for peace of mind, confidence, and security, around the world or just around the corner.

do more ®

AMERICAN EXPRESS

Cards

In case you're running low.

We're here to help with more than 118,000 Express Cash locations around the world. In order to enroll, just call American Express before you start your vacation.

do more

AMERICAN EXPRESS

Express Cash

Old Town Bridge Tower. This was where Peter Parler (the architect of St. Vitus Cathedral) began his bridge building. The carved facades he designed for the sides of the bridge were destroyed by Swedish soldiers in 1648, at the end of the Thirty Years' War. The sculptures facing the square, however, are still intact; they depict an old and gout-ridden Charles IV with his son, who later became Wenceslas IV. ▧ *20 Kč.* ☉ *Daily 9–7.*

㉙ Schönbornský palác (Schönborn Palace). Franz Kafka had an apartment in this massive baroque building at the top of Tržiště ulice from March through August 1917, after moving out from Zlatá ulička (Golden Lane) (☞ Prague Castle, *below*). The U.S. Embassy now occupies this prime location. If you look through the gates, you can see the beautiful formal gardens rising up to the Petřín hill; they are unfortunately not open to the public. ✉ *Tržiště at Vlašská.*

U tří pštrosů (the Three Ostriches). The original building stems from the 16th century, when one of the early owners was a supplier of ostrich feathers to the royal court and had the house's three unmistakable emblems painted on the facade. The top floors and curlicue gables were early baroque additions from the 17th century. The ancient inn functions as a hotel to this day. It was the site of the first coffeehouse in Prague, opened by the Armenian Deodat Damajian in 1714. ✉ *Dražického nám. 12.*

NEED A BREAK? At the corner of Na Kampě, right next to the arches of the Charles Bridge, the small stand-up café **Bistro Bruncvík** serves hot wine and coffee in winter and cold drinks in summer. Its slices of pizza are also satisfying.

㉜ Velkopřevorské náměstí (Grand Priory Square). The palace fronting the square is considered one of the finest baroque buildings in the Malá Strana, though it is now part of the Embassy of the Knights of Malta and no longer open to the public. Opposite is the flamboyant orange-and-white stucco facade of the Buquoy Palace, built in 1719 by Giovanni Santini and the present home of the French Embassy. From the street you can glimpse an enormous twinkling chandelier through the window, but this is about all you'll get to see of the elegant interior.

㉟ Vojanovy sady. Once the gardens of the Monastery of the Discalced Carmelites, later taken over by the Order of the English Virgins and now part of the Ministry of Finance, this walled garden, with its weeping willows, fruit trees, and benches, makes another peaceful haven in summer. Exhibitions of modern sculptures are often held here, contrasting sharply with the two baroque chapels and the graceful Ignaz Platzer statue of John of Nepomuk standing on a fish at the entrance. The park is surrounded by the high walls of the old monastery and Ministry of Finance buildings, with only an occasional glimpse of a tower or spire to remind you that you're in Prague. ⊠ *U lužického semináře, between Letenská and Míšeňská Sts.* ☉ *Daily 8–5 (until 7 in summer).*

㉚ Vrtbovský palác (Vrtba Palace and Gardens). An unobtrusive door on noisy Karmelitská hides the entranceway to an intimate courtyard. Walk between the two Renaissance houses, the one to the left built in 1575, the one to the right in 1591. The owner of the latter house was one of the 27 Bohemian nobles executed by the Hapsburgs in 1621 before the Old Town Hall. The house was given as confiscated property to Count Sezima of Vrtba, who bought the neighboring property and turned the buildings into a late-Renaissance palace. The Vrtbovská zahrada (Vrtba Gardens), created a century later, boasts one of the best views over the Malá Strana rooftops and is a fascinating oasis from the tourist beat. Unfortunately, the gardens are perpetually closed for renovation, even though there is no sign of work in progress. The powerful stone figure of Atlas that caps the entranceway dates from 1720 and is the work of Mathias Braun. ⊠ *Karmelitská ul. 25.*

OFF THE BEATEN PATH

VILLA BERTRAMKA – Mozart fans won't want to pass up a visit to this villa, where the great composer lived when in Prague. The small, well-organized museum is packed with memorabilia, including the program from that exciting night in 1787 when *Don Giovanni* had its world premiere in Prague. Also on hand is one of the master's pianos. Take Tram 12 from Karmelitská south to the Anděl metro station (or ride metro Line B), walk down Plzeňská ulice a few hundred yards, and take a left at Mozartova ulice. ⊠ *Mozartova ul. 169, Smíchov,* ☎ *02/543893.* 🎟 *60Kč.* ⊙ *Daily 10–5.*

★ ㊱ **Zahrada Valdštejnského paláca** (Wallenstein Palace Gardens). Albrecht von Wallenstein, onetime owner of the house and gardens, began a meteoric military career in 1624 when the Austrian emperor Ferdinand II retained him to save the empire from the Swedes and Protestants during the Thirty Years' War. Wallenstein, wealthy by marriage, offered to raise 20,000 men at his own cost and lead them personally. Ferdinand II accepted and showered Wallenstein with confiscated land and titles. Wallenstein's first acquisition was this enormous area. Having knocked down 23 houses, a brick factory, and three gardens, in 1623 he began to build his magnificent palace with its idiosyncratic high-walled gardens and superb Renaissance *sala terrena.* Walking around the formal paths, you'll come across numerous statues, an unusual fountain with a woman spouting water from her breasts, and a lava-stone grotto along the wall. Most of the palace itself is earmarked to serve the Czech Senate. The only part open to the public, the cavernous *Jízdárna,* or riding school (not to be confused with the Prague Castle Riding School), hosts occasional art exhibitions. ⊠ *Garden entrance at Letenská 10.* 🎟 *Free.* ⊙ *May–Sept., daily 9–7.*

THE CASTLE DISTRICT

To the west of Prague Castle is the residential **Hradčany** (Castle District), the town that during the early 14th century emerged out of a collection of monasteries and churches. The concentration of history packed into one small area makes Prague Castle and the Castle District challenging objects for visitors not versed in the ups and downs of Bohemian kings, religious uprisings, wars, and oppression. The picturesque area surrounding Prague Castle, with its breathtaking vistas of the Old Town and Malá Strana, is ideal for just wandering; but the castle itself, with its convoluted history and architecture, is difficult to appreciate fully without investing a little more time.

A Good Walk

Numbers in the text correspond to numbers in the margin and on the Exploring Prague map.

Begin on **Nerudova ulice** ㉗, which runs east–west a few hundred yards south of Prague Castle. At the western foot of the street, look for a flight of stone steps guarded by two saintly statues. The stairs lead up to Loretánská ulice, affording panoramic views of St. Nicholas Church and Malá Strana. At the top of the steps, turn left and walk a couple hundred yards until you come to a dusty elongated square named **Pohořelec** ㊲. Go through the inconspicuous gateway at No. 8 and up the steps, and you'll find yourself in the courtyard of one of the city's richest monasteries, the **Strahovský klášter** ㊳.

Retrace your steps to Loretánské náměstí, which is flanked by the feminine curves of the baroque **Loreto Church** ㊴. Across the road, the 29 half pillars of the **Černínský palác** now mask the Czech Ministry of Foreign Affairs. At the bottom of Loretánské náměstí, a little lane trails to the left into the area known as **Nový Svět**; the name means "new world," though the district is as Old World as they come. Turn right onto the street Nový Svět. Around the corner you get a tantalizing view of the cathedral through the trees. Walk past the Austrian Embassy to Kanovnická ulice, a winding street lined with the dignified but melancholy **Kostel svatého Jana Nepomuckého.** At the top of the street on the left, the rounded, Renaissance corner house **Martinický palác** (Martinic Palace) catches the eye with its detailed sgraffito drawings. Martinic Palace opens onto **Hradčanské náměstí** ㊵ with its grandiose gathering of Renaissance and baroque palaces. To the left of the bright yellow Archbishop's Palace on the square is an alleyway leading down to the **Národní galérie** ㊶ and its collections of European art. Across the square, the handsome sgraffito sweep of **Schwarzenberg palác** ㊷ beckons; this is the building you saw from the back side at the beginning of the tour.

TIMING

Brisk-paced sightseers could zip through Hradčany in an hour, but to do it justice, allow at least an hour just for ambling and admiring the passing buildings and views of the city. The Strahov Monastery's halls need about a half hour

The Castle District

to take in, and the Loreto Church and its treasures at least that length of time. The National Gallery in the Šternberský palá deserves at least a couple of hours.

Sights to See

Černínský palác (Chernin Palace). While the Loreto Church (☞ *below*) represents the softer side of the Counter-Reformation, this ungainly, overbearing structure seems to stand for the harsh political fate that met the Czechs after their defeat at the battle of Bílá Hora in 1620. During World War II it was the seat of the occupying German government.

㊵ Hradčanské náměstí (Hradčany Square). With its fabulous mixture of baroque and Renaissance housing, topped by the castle itself, the square featured prominently (ironically, disguised as Vienna) in the film *Amadeus*, directed by the then-exiled Czech director Miloš Forman. The house at No. 7 was the set for Mozart's residence, where the composer was haunted by the masked figure he thought was his father. Forman used the flamboyant rococo **Arcibiskupský palác** (Archbishop's Palace), at the top of the square on the left, as the Viennese archbishop's palace. The plush interior, shown off in the film, is open to the public only on Maundy Thursday.

㊴ Loreto Church. The church's seductive lines were a conscious move on the part of Counter-Reformation Jesuits in the 17th century who wanted to build up the cult of Mary and attract the largely Protestant Bohemians back to the church. According to legend, angels had carried Mary's house in Nazareth and dropped it in a patch of laurel trees in Ancona, Italy; known as *Loreto* (from the Latin for laurel), it immediately became a center of pilgrimage. The Prague Loreto was one of many re-creations of this scene across Europe, and it worked: Pilgrims came in droves. The graceful facade, with its voluptuous tower, was built in 1720 by Kilian Ignaz Dientzenhofer, the architect of the two St. Nicholas churches in Prague. Most spectacular of all is a small exhibition upstairs displaying the religious treasures presented to Mary in thanks for various services, including a monstrance studded with 6,500 diamonds. ✉ *Loretánské nám. 7,* ☎ *02/2451–0789.* 🎫 *30 Kč.* ☉ *Tues.–Sun. 9–12:15 and 1–4:30.*

★ **㊶ Národní galérie** (National Gallery); housed in the 18th-century Šternberský palác (Sternberg Palace). You'll need at least an hour to view the palace's impressive art collection—one collection in Prague you should not miss. On the first floor there's an exhibition of icons and other religious art from the 3rd through the 14th centuries. Up a second flight of steps is an entire room full of Cranachs and an assortment of paintings by Holbein, Dürer, Brueghel, Van Dyck, Canaletto, and Rubens. Other branches of the National Gallery are scattered around town, notably, the modern art collections in the Veletržní palác (☞ Letná and Holešovice, *below*). ⊠ *Hradčanské nám. 15,* ☏ *02/2451–0594.* ⌨ *50 Kč.* ☉ *Tues.–Sun. 10–6.*

Nový Svět. This picturesque, winding little alley, with facades from the 17th and 18th centuries, once housed Prague's poorest residents; now many of the homes are used as artists' studios. The last house on the street, No. 1, was the home of the Danish-born astronomer Tycho Brahe. Living so close to the Loreto, so the story goes, Tycho was constantly disturbed during his nightly stargazing by the church bells. He ended up complaining to his patron, Emperor Rudolf II, who instructed the Capuchin monks to finish their services before the first star appeared in the sky.

㊲ Pohořelec (Scene of Fire). This area suffered tragic fires in 1420, 1541, and 1741. The 1541 calamity sparked into life on Malostranské náměstí and spread up the hill, ravaging much of Malá Strana and the castle as it raged. Many Gothic houses burned down, opening up large plots for the Renaissance and especially the baroque houses and palaces that dominate the quarter's architectural face.

㊷ Schwarzenberský palác (Schwarzenberg Palace). This boxy palace with its extravagant sgraffito facade was built for the Lobkowicz family between 1545 and 1563; today it houses the **Vojenské historické muzeum** (Military History Museum), one of the largest of its kind in Europe. Of more general interest are the jousting tournaments held in the courtyard in summer. ⊠ *Hradčanské nám. 2.* ⌨ *20 Kč.* ☉ *Apr.–Oct., Tues.–Sun. 10–6.*

★ **㊳ Strahovský klášter** (Strahov Monastery). Founded by the Premonstratensian order in 1140, the monastery remained in their hands until 1952, when the Communists abolished all religious orders and turned the entire complex into the **Památník národního písemnictví** (Museum of National Literature). The major building of interest is the **Strahov Library,** with its collection of early Czech manuscripts, the 10th-century Strahov New Testament, and the collected works of famed Danish astronomer Tycho Brahe. Also of note is the late-18th-century **Philosophical Hall.** Engulfing its ceilings is a startling sky-blue fresco completed by the Austrian painter Franz Anton Maulbertsch in just six months. The fresco depicts an unusual cast of characters, including Socrates' nagging wife Xanthippe, Greek astronomer Thales with his trusty telescope, and a collection of Greek philosophers mingling with Descartes, Diderot, and Voltaire. ⊠ *Strahovské nádvoří 1/132.* 🎫 *20 Kč.* ☼ *Daily 9–noon and 1–5.*

> **OFF THE BEATEN PATH**
>
> **PETŘÍN –** For a superb view of the city—from a mostly undiscovered, tourist-free perch—stroll over from the Strahov Monastery along the paths toward Prague's own miniature version of the Eiffel Tower. The tower and its breathtaking view, the hall of mirrors, and the seemingly abandoned church are beautifully peaceful and well worth an afternoon's wandering. You can also walk up from Karmelitská ulice or Újezd down in Malá Strana or ride the funicular railway from U lanové dráhy ulice, off Újezd. Regular public-transportation tickets are valid. For the descent, take the funicular or meander on foot down through the stations of the cross on the pathways leading back to Malá Strana.

LETNÁ AND HOLEŠOVICE

From above the Vltava's left bank, the large grassy plateau called Letná affords one of the classic views of the Old Town and the many bridges crossing the river. Beer gardens, tennis, and Frisbee attract people of all ages, while amateur soccer players emulate the professionals of Prague's top team, Sparta, which plays in the stadium just across the road. Ten minutes' walk from Letná, down into the residential neighborhood of Holešovice, brings you to a massive, gray-blue pile of a building that might have been designed by a young postmodernist architect. In fact it dates to the 1920s, and the cool exterior gives no hint of the cavernous halls within or of the treasures of Czech and French modern art that line its corridors. Just north along Dukelských hrdinů Street, Stromovka—a royal hunting preserve turned gracious park—offers quiet strolls under huge old oaks and chestnuts.

Numbers in the margin correspond to numbers on the Exploring Prague map.

㊸ Letenské sady (Letna Gardens). Come to this large, shady park for an unforgettable view from on high of Prague's bridges. From the enormous cement pedestal at the center of the park, the largest statue of Stalin in Eastern Europe once beckoned to citizens on the Old Town Square far below. The statue was ripped down in the 1960s, when Stalinism was finally discredited. The walks and grass that stretch out behind the pedestal are perfect for relaxing on a warm afternoon. On sunny Sundays expatriates often meet up here to play ultimate Frisbee. ✉ *Prague 7. To get to Letna, cross the Čechův Bridge, opposite the Hotel Inter-Continental, and climb the stairs.*

㊹ Veletržní palác Museum of Modern Art. The National Gallery's newest museum, housed in a trade-fair hall in the Holešovice neighborhood, set off a furor when it opened in 1995. The lighting, the exhibit design, the unused empty spaces in the building's two enormous halls, even the selection of paintings and sculpture—all came under critics' scrutiny. The negative voices couldn't deny, though, that the palace—itself a key work of constructivist architecture—serves a vital purpose in making permanently accessible hundreds of pieces of 20th-century Czech art. Much of the collections languished in storage for decades, either because some cultural commissar forbade its public display or for simple lack of exhibition space. The collection of 19th- and 20th-century French art, including an important group of early cubist paintings by Picasso and Braque, is also here, moved from the Šternberský Palace. ✉ *Veletržní at Dukelských hrdinů, Prague 7.* 💰 *80 Kč.* ☉ *Tues.–Sun. 10–6.*

| OFF THE BEATEN PATH | **ZOOLOGICKÁ ZAHRADA** – Prague's small but delightful zoo is north of the city in Troja, under the shadow of the Troja Castle. Take the metro Line C to Nádraží Holešovice and change to Bus 112. ⊠ *U trojského zámku 3, Prague 7,* ☎ *02/688-0480.* ⊠ *30 Kč.* ⊙ *May–Sept., daily 9–6; Oct.–Apr., daily 9–4.* |

VINOHRADY

From Riegrovy sady and its sweeping view of the city from above the National Museum, the elegant residential neighborhood called Vinohrady extends its streets of eclectic apartment houses and villas eastward and southward. The pastel-tinted ranks of turn-of-the-century apartment houses—many crumbling after years of neglect—are slowly but unstoppably being transformed into upscale flats, slick offices, eternally packed new restaurants, and a range of shops unthinkable only a half decade ago. Much of the development lies on or near Vinohradská, the main street, which extends from the top of Wenceslas Square to a belt of enormous cemeteries about 2 miles eastward. Yet the flavor of daily life persists: Smoky old pubs still ply their trade on the quiet side streets; the stately theater, Divadlo na Vinohradech, keeps putting on excellent shows as it has for decades; and on the squares and in the parks nearly everyone still practices Prague's favorite form of outdoor exercise—walking the dog.

㊺ Kostel Nejsvětějšího Srdce Páně (Church of the Most Sacred Heart). If you've had your fill of Romanesque, Gothic, and baroque, take the metro to the Jiřího z Poděbrad station (Line A) for a look at a startling art-deco edifice. Designed in 1927 by Slovenian architect Josip Plečnik (the same architect commissioned to update Prague Castle), the church resembles a luxury ocean liner more than a place of worship. The effect was conscious; during the 1920s and '30s, the avantgarde imitated mammoth objects of modern technology. Plečnik used many modern elements on the inside: Notice the hanging speakers, seemingly designed to bring the word of God directly to the ears of each worshiper. You may be able to find someone at the back entrance of the church who will let you walk up the long ramp into the fascinating glass clock tower. ⊠ *Nám. Jiřího z Poděbrad, Prague 3.*

㊻ Židovské hřbitovy (New Jewish Cemetery). Tens of thousands of Czechs find eternal rest in Vinohrady's cemeteries. The modest **tombstone of Franz Kafka** in the newest of the city's half-dozen Jewish cemeteries, situated where Vinohrady's elegance peters out into more mundane districts, seems grossly inadequate to Kafka's stature but oddly in proportion to his own modest ambitions. The cemetery is usually open for visitors, although guards sometimes inexplicably seal off the grounds. Turn right at the main cemetery gate and follow the wall for about 100 yards. Dr. Franz Kafka's thin, white tombstone lies at the front of Section 21. ✉ *Vinohradská at Jana Želivského, Prague 3 (metro station Želivského).* 🎫 *Free.* ⏰ *Summer, Sun.–Thurs. 8–5; winter Sun.–Thurs. 9–4 (closes at 3 on Sun. in winter).*

A much smaller, but older, Jewish burial ground huddles at the foot of the soaring rocket ship–like television tower that broke ground in the last years of communism and used to be dubbed, in mockery, "Big Brother's Finger." The cemetery once spread where the tower now stands, but Jewish community leaders agreed, or were pressured, into letting it be dug up and the most historic tombstones crammed into one corner of the large square. The stones date back as far as the 17th century; a little neoclassical mausoleum stands forlornly just outside the fence. The cemetery gate is almost never unlocked. ✉ *Fibichova at Kubelíkova, Prague 3.*

PRAGUE CASTLE

Numbers in the text correspond to numbers in the margin and on the Prague Castle (Pražský hrad) map.

Despite its monolithic presence, Pražský hrad (Prague Castle) is a collection of buildings dating from the 10th to the 20th centuries, all linked by internal courtyards. The most important structures are **Chrám svatého Víta** (St. Vitus Cathedral) ㊷, clearly visible soaring above the castle walls, and the **Královský palác** (Royal Palace) ㊵, the official residence of kings and presidents and still the center of political power in the Czech Republic. The castle is compact and easy to navigate in. Visitors can easily design a walking tour to fit their interests and the time they have for sightseeing. Be forewarned: In summer, St. Vitus Cathedral and Golden

Lane take the brunt of the heavy sightseeing traffic, while all of the castle is hugely popular.

TIMING

The castle is at its mysterious best in early morning and late evening, and it is incomparable when it snows. You can charge through the castle in 10 minutes, but that would be criminal. The cathedral deserves an hour, as does the Royal Palace, while you can easily spend an entire day taking in the many other museums and their architectural details, the views of the city, and the hidden nooks of the castle.

Sights to See

Bazilika svatého Jiří (St. George's Basilica). This church was originally built in the 10th century by Prince Vratislav I, the father of Prince (and St.) Wenceslas. It was dedicated to St. George (of dragon fame), who it was believed would be more agreeable to the still largely pagan people. The outside was remodeled during early baroque times, although the striking rusty-red color is in keeping with the look of the Romanesque edifice. The interior, following substantial renovation, looks more or less as it did in the 12th century and is the best-preserved Romanesque relic in the country. The effect is at once barnlike and peaceful, the warm golden yellow of the stone walls and the small triplet arched windows exuding a sense of enduring harmony. The house-shaped, painted tomb at the front of the church holds the remains of the founder, Vratislav I. Up the steps, in a chapel to the right, is the tomb Parler designed for St. Ludmila, the grandmother of St. Wenceslas. ☒ *Náměstí U sv. Jiří.*

Castle Information Office. Empress Maria Theresa's court architect, Nicolò Pacassi, received the imperial approval to remake the castle in the 1760s. The castle took heavy damage from Prussian shelling during the War of the Austrian Succession in 1757. The **Druhé nádvoří** (Second Courtyard) was the main victim of his attempts at imparting classical grandeur to what had been a picturesque collection of Gothic and Renaissance styles. Except for the view of the spires of St. Vitus Cathedral towering above the palace, there's little for the eye to feast upon here. The main reason to come is to visit the main castle information office for entrance tickets, headphones for listening to recorded tours, tickets to cultural events, and changing money. ☒ *Druhé nádvoří.*

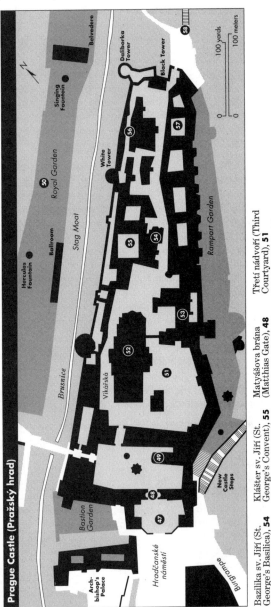

Tickets (80 Kč, valid for 3 consecutive days) give admission to older parts of St. Vitus Cathedral, Royal Palace, St. George's Basilica, and Mihulka Tower. ☉ These sites open Nov.–Mar., daily 9–5; Apr.–Oct., daily 9–4. Castle gardens Apr.–Oct., Tues.–Sun. 10–6 (free admission).

The Second Courtyard also houses the reliquary of Charles IV inside the **Kaple svatého Kříže** (Chapel of the Holy Cross). Displays include Gothic silver busts of the major Bohemian patron saints and bones and vestments that supposedly belonged to various saints.

Built in the late-16th and early 17th centuries, the Second Courtyard was part of a reconstruction program commissioned by Rudolf II, under whom Prague enjoyed a period of unparalleled cultural development. Once the Prague court was established, the emperor gathered around him some of the world's best craftsmen, artists, and scientists, including the brilliant astronomers Johannes Kepler and Tycho Brahe.

Rudolf also amassed a large collection of art, surveying instruments, and coins. The bulk of the collection was looted by the Swedes and Hapsburgs during the Thirty Years' War or auctioned off during the 18th century, but a small part of the collection was rediscovered in unused castle rooms in the 1960s. It used to be displayed, and will be again when slow-moving repairs are completed, in the **Obrazárna** (Picture Gallery), on the left side of the Second Courtyard. The passageway at the gallery entrance forms the northern entrance to the castle and leads out over a luxurious ravine known as the **Jelení příkop** (Stag Moat).

★ ⓬ **Chrám svatého Víta** (St. Vitus Cathedral). With its graceful, soaring towers, this Gothic cathedral—among the most beautiful in Europe—is the spiritual heart of Prague Castle, the city itself, and all of the Czech Republic. It has a long and complicated history, beginning in the 10th century and continuing to its completion in 1929. If you want to hear its history in depth, English-speaking guided tours of the cathedral and the Royal Palace (☞ *below*) can be arranged at the information office in the castle's Second Courtyard.

Once you enter the cathedral, pause to take in the vast but delicate beauty of the Gothic and neo-Gothic interior glowing in the colorful light that filters through the startlingly brilliant stained-glass windows. This back half, including the western facade and the two towers you can see from outside, was not completed until 1929, following the initiative of the Union for the Completion of the Cathedral set up in the last days of the 19th century. Don't let the neo-Gothic delusion keep you from examining this new section. The six stained-glass windows to your left and right and the large rose window behind are modern masterpieces. Take a good look at the third window up on the left. The familiar art-nouveau flamboyance, depicting the blessing of the 9th-century St. Cyril and St. Methodius (missionaries to the Slavs and creators of the Cyrillic alphabet), is the work of the Czech father of the style, Alfons Mucha. He achieved the subtle coloring by painting rather than staining the glass.

If you walk halfway up the right-hand aisle (and you've bought a Prague Castle sightseeing ticket, which permits you to enter the older parts of the cathedral (☞ Castle Information Office, *above*), you will find the exquisitely ornate **Chapel of St. Válav (Wenceslas).** With a 14th-century tomb holding the saint's remains, this square chapel is the ancient heart of the cathedral. Wenceslas (the "good king" of Christmas-carol fame) was a determined Christian in an era of widespread paganism. In 925, as prince of Bohemia, he founded a rotunda church dedicated to St. Vitus on this site. But the prince's brother, Boleslav, was impatient to take power and ambushed Wenceslas four years later near a church at Stará Boleslav, northeast of Prague. Wenceslas was originally buried in that church, but his grave produced so many miracles that he rapidly became a symbol of piety for the common people, something that greatly irritated the new Prince Boleslav. In 931 Boleslav was finally forced to honor his brother by reburying the body in the St. Vitus Rotunda. Shortly afterward, Wenceslas was canonized.

The rotunda was replaced by a Romanesque basilica in the late 11th century. Work was begun on the existing building in 1344, on the initiative of the man who was later to become Charles IV. For the first few years the chief architect was the Frenchman Mathias d'Arras, but after his death in 1352, the work was continued by the 22-year-old German architect Peter Parler, who went on to build the Charles Bridge and many other Prague treasures.

The small door in the back of the chapel leads to the **Crown Chamber,** the repository of the Bohemian crown jewels. It remains locked with seven keys held by seven different people and is definitely not open to the public.

A little beyond the Wenceslas Chapel on the same side, stairs lead down to the underground **royal crypt,** interesting primarily for the information it provides about the cathedral's history. As you descend the stairs, on the right you'll see parts of the old Romanesque basilica. A little farther, in a niche to the left, are portions of the foundations of the rotunda. Moving around into the second room, you'll find a rather eclectic group of royal remains ensconced in new sarcophagi dating from the 1930s. In the center is Charles IV, who died in 1378. Rudolf II, patron of Renaissance Prague, is entombed at the rear in the original tin coffin. To his right is Maria Amalia, the only child of Maria Theresa to reside in Prague. Ascending the wooden steps back into the cathedral, you'll come to the white-marble **Royal Mausoleum,** atop which lie stone statues of the first two Hapsburg kings to rule in Bohemia, Ferdinand I and Maximilian II.

The cathedral's **Royal Oratory** was used by the kings and their families when attending mass. Built in 1493, the work is a perfect example of late Gothic, laced on the outside with a stone network of gnarled branches very similar in pattern to the ceiling vaulting in the Royal Palace (☞ *below*). The oratory is connected to the palace by an elevated covered walkway, which you can see from outside.

From here you can't fail to catch sight of the ornate silver **sarcophagus of St. John of Nepomuk,** designed by the famous Viennese architect Fischer von Erlach. According to legend, when Nepomuk's body was exhumed in 1721 to be reinterred, the tongue was found to be still intact and pumping with blood. These strange tales sadly served a highly political purpose. The Catholic Church and the Hapsburgs were seeking a new folk hero to replace the Protestant Jan Hus, whom they despised. The late Father Nepomuk was sainted and reburied a few years later with great ceremony in the 3,700-pound silver tomb, replete with angels and cherubim; the tongue was enshrined in its own reliquary.

The eight chapels around the back of the cathedral are the work of the original architect, Mathias d'Arras. A number of old tombstones, including some badly worn grave markers of medieval royalty, can be seen within, amid furnishings from later periods. Opposite the wooden relief, depicting the looting of the cathedral by Protestants in 1619, is the **Wallenstein Chapel**. Since the last century, it has housed the Gothic tombstones of its two architects, Mathias d'Arras and Peter Parler, who died in 1352 and 1399, respectively. If you look up to the balcony, you can just make out the busts of these two men, designed by Parler's workshop. The other busts around the triforium depict various Czech kings.

The Hussite wars in the 15th century put an end to the first phase of the cathedral's construction. During the short era of illusory peace before the Thirty Years' War, lack of money laid to rest any idea of finishing the building, and the cathedral was closed by a wall built across from the Wenceslas Chapel. Not until the 20th century was the western side of the cathedral, with its two towers, completed according to Parler's original plans. ⊠ *St. Vitus Cathedral.* *Free admission to the western part. Chapels, crypt, and tower accessible with castle-wide ticket.* ⊙ *May–Sept., daily 9–5; Oct.–Apr., daily 9–4.*

㊺ Klášter svatého Jiří (St. George's Convent). The first convent in Bohemia, founded in 973 next to the even older St. George's Basilica, now houses the Old Bohemian Collection of the **Czech National Gallery**. The museum runs through the history of Czech art from the early Middle Ages, with exhibits that include religious statues, icons, and triptychs, to the rather more secular themes of the Mannerist school and the voluptuous work of the court painters of Rudolf II. ⊠ *Nám. U sv. Jiří,* ☎ *02/2451–0695.* *50 Kč.* ⊙ *Tues.–Sun. 10–6.*

㊿ Královská zahrada (Royal Garden). This peaceful swath of greenery affords an unusually lovely view of St. Vitus Cathedral and the castle's walls and bastions. Originally laid out in the 16th century, it endured devastation in war, neglect in times of peace, and many redesigns, reaching its present parklike form early this century. Luckily, its Renaissance treasures survive. The garden front of the **Míčovna** (Ball Game Hall), built by Bonifaz Wohlmut in 1568, is completely covered by a dense tangle of allegorical sgraffiti; it was restored in the 1970s after fading to near invisibility.

The **Královský letohrádek** (Royal Summer Palace, also known as the Belvedere), at the garden's eastern end, deserves its usual description as "one of the most beautiful Renaissance structures north of the Alps." Italian architects began it; Wohlmut finished it off in the 1560s with a copper roof like an upturned boat's keel riding above the graceful arcades of the ground floor. In the 18th and 19th centuries, military engineers tested artillery in the interior, which had already lost its rich furnishings to Swedish soldiers during their siege of the city in 1648. The Renaissance-style *giardinetto* (little garden) adjoining the summer palace centers around another masterwork, the Italian-designed, Czech-cast *Singing Fountain*, which resonates to the sound of falling water. ✉ *Garden entrances from U Prašného mostu ul. and Mariánské hradby ul. near Chotkovy Sady Park.* 🎫 *Free.* ⊘ *Apr.–Oct., Tues.–Sun. 10–5:45.*

❺ **Královský palác** (Royal Palace). There are two main points of interest inside the externally nondescript palace. The first is the **Vladislavský sál** (Vladislav Hall), the largest secular Gothic interior space in Central Europe. The enormous hall was completed in 1493 by Benedict Ried, who was to late-Bohemian Gothic what Peter Parler was to the earlier version. The room imparts a sense of space and light, softened by the sensuous lines of the vaulted ceilings and brought to a dignified close by the simple oblong form of the early Renaissance windows, a style that was just beginning to make inroads in Central Europe. In its heyday, the hall was the site of jousting tournaments, festive markets, banquets, and coronations. In more recent times, it has been used to inaugurate presidents, from the Communist Klement Gottwald in 1948 to Václav Havel in 1990.

From the front of the hall, turn right into the rooms of the **Česká kancelář** (Bohemian Chancellery). This wing was built by the same Benedict Ried only 10 years after the hall was completed, but it shows a much stronger Renaissance influence. Pass through the Renaissance portal into the last chamber of the chancellery. This room was the site of the second defenestration of Prague, in 1618, an event that marked the beginning of the Bohemian rebellion and, ultimately, of the Thirty Years' War. This peculiarly Bohemian method of expressing protest (throwing someone out a window) had first been used in 1419 in the New Town Hall, an event that led to the Hussite wars. Two hundred years later the same conflict was reexpressed in terms of Hapsburg-backed Catholics versus Bohemian Protestants. Rudolf II had reached an uneasy agreement with the Bohemian nobles, allowing them religious freedom in exchange for financial support. But his successor, Ferdinand II, was a rabid opponent of Protestantism and disregarded Rudolf's tolerant "Letter of Majesty." Enraged, the Protestant nobles stormed the castle and chancellery and threw two Catholic officials and their secretary, for good measure, out the window. Legend has it they landed on a mound of horse dung and escaped unharmed, an event the Jesuits interpreted as a miracle. The square window in question is on the left as you enter the room.

At the back of the Vladislav Hall, a staircase leads up to a gallery of the **All Saints' Chapel.** Little remains of Peter Parler's original work, but the church contains some fine works of art. The large room to the left of the staircase is the **Stará sněmovna** (council chamber), where the Bohemian nobles met with the king in a kind of prototype parliament. Portraits of the Hapsburg rulers line the walls. The descent from Vladislav Hall toward what remains of the **Romanesque palace** is by way of a wide, shallow set of steps. This **Riders' Staircase** was the entranceway for knights who came for the jousting tournaments. ✉ *Royal Palác, Třetí nádvoří.*

㊼ Lobkovický palác (Lobkowicz Palace). From the beginning of the 17th century until the 1940s, this building was the residence of the powerful Catholic Lobkowicz family. It was to this house that the two defenestrated officials escaped after landing on the dung hill in 1618. During the 1970s the building was restored to its early baroque appearance and now houses the permanent exhibition "Monuments of the Czech National Past." If you want to get a chronological understanding of Czech history from the beginnings of the Great Moravian Empire in the 9th century to the Czech national uprising in 1848, this is the place. Copies of the crown jewels are on display here; but it is the rich collection of illuminated Bibles, old musical instruments, coins, weapons, royal decrees, paintings, and statues that makes the museum well worth visiting. Detailed information on the exhibits is available in English. ✉ *Jiřská ul.* 🎫 *30 Kč.* ⊙ *Tues.–Sun. 9–5.*

㊽ Matyášova brána (Matthias Gate). Built in 1614, the stone gate once stood alone in front of the moats and bridges that surrounded the castle. Under the Hapsburgs, the gate survived by being grafted as a relief onto the palace building. As you go through it, notice the ceremonial white-marble entrance halls on either side, which lead up to President Václav Havel's reception rooms (only rarely open to the public).

㊼ První nádvoří (First Courtyard). The main entrance to Prague Castle from Hradčanské náměstí is a little disappointing. Going through the wrought-iron gate, guarded at ground level by pristine Czech soldiers and from above by the ferocious *Battling Titans* (a copy of Ignaz Platzer's original 18th-century statues), you'll enter this courtyard, built on the site of old moats and gates that once separated the castle from the surrounding buildings and thus protected the vulnerable western flank. The courtyard is one of the more recent additions to the castle, designed by Maria Theresa's court architect, Nicolò Pacassi, in the 1760s. Today it forms part of the presidential office complex. Pacassi's reconstruction was intended to unify the eclectic collection of buildings that made up the castle. From a distance, the effect is monumental. As you move farther into the castle, large parts appear to be relatively new, while in reality they cover splendid Gothic and Romanesque interiors.

㊾ Staré zámecké schody (Old Castle Steps). Unending lines of tourists pass by dozens of trinket sellers and, in recent years, more and more beggars as they troop up and down this long walled staircase. It starts from the castle's Black Tower and comes out just above the Malostranská metro station. There you can catch the subway or take a tram toward Malostranské náměstí.

㊿ Třetí nádvoří (Third Courtyard). The contrast between the cool, dark interior of the cathedral and the brightly colored Pacassi facades of the Third Courtyard just outside is startling. The courtyard's clean lines are the work of Slovenian architect Josip Plečnik in the 1930s, but the modern look is a deception. Plečnik's paving was intended to cover an underground world of wooden houses, streets, and walls dating from the 9th through the 12th centuries—rediscovered when the cathedral was completed. Since these are not open to the public, we are left with the modern structure (supplemented recently by an exchange office). Plečnik did add a few eclectic features to catch the eye: a granite obelisk to commemorate the fallen of the First World War, a black-marble pedestal for the Gothic statue of St. George (the original is in the museum at St. George's Convent), and the peculiar golden ball topping the eagle fountain near the eastern end of the courtyard.

㊶ Zlatá ulička (Golden Lane). An enchanting collection of tiny, ancient, brightly colored houses crouches under the fortification wall looking remarkably like a Disney set for *Snow White and the Seven Dwarfs*. Legend has it that these were the lodgings of the international group of alchemists whom Rudolf II brought to the court to produce gold. The truth is a little less romantic: The houses were built during the 16th century for the castle guards, who supplemented their income by practicing various crafts outside the jurisdiction of the powerful guilds. By the early 20th century, Golden Lane had become the home of poor artists and writers. Franz Kafka, who lived at No. 22 in 1916 and 1917, described the house on first sight as "so small, so dirty, impossible to live in and lacking everything necessary." But he soon came to love the place. As he wrote to his fiancée: "Life here is something special . . . to close out the world not just by shutting the door to a room or apartment but to the whole house, to step out into the snow of the silent lane." The lane now houses tiny stores selling books, music, and crafts.

3 Dining

DINING CHOICES IN PRAGUE have increased greatly in the past year as hundreds of new places have opened to cope with the increased tourist demand. Quality and price vary widely, though. Be wary of tourist traps; cross-check prices of foreign-language menus with Czech versions. Also ask if there is a *denní lístek* (daily menu). These menus, usually written only in Czech, generally list cheaper and often fresher selections (though many places provide daily menus for the midday meal only).

The crush of visitors has placed tremendous strain on the more popular restaurants. The upshot: Reservations are nearly always required; this is especially true during peak tourist periods. If you don't have reservations, try arriving a little before standard meal times: 11:30 AM for lunch or 5:30 PM for dinner.

For a cheaper and quicker alternative to the sit-down establishments listed below, try a light meal at one of the city's growing number of street stands and fast-food places. Look for stands offering *párky* (hot dogs) or *smažený syr* (fried cheese). McDonald's, with several locations in the city, heads the list of Western imports. For more exotic fare, try a gyro (made from pork) at the stand on the Staroměstské náměstí or the very good vegetarian fare at **Country Life** (✉ Melantrichova ul. 15, ☏ 02/2421–3366), open Sunday to Friday. The German coffeemaker **Tchibo** has teamed up with a local bakery and now offers tasty sandwiches and excellent coffee at convenient locations on the Staroměstské náměstí and at the top of Wenceslas Square.

CATEGORY	PRICE*
$$$$	over $25
$$$	$15–$25
$$	$7–$15
$	under $7

per person for a three-course meal, excluding wine and tip

Old Town

$$$$ ✕ **Potomac.** Chef Jörn Heinrich lends imagination and creativity to Potomac's fresh imported ingredients, and dis-

cerning diners can't ask for anything more. The two-pepper soup proves a superb starter for main courses of grilled sea bass, and beef fillet with roasted cashews, green beans, and kidney beans. ⊠ *Renaissance Hotel, V celnici 7, Prague 1 (near Námûstí Republiky),* ☏ *02/2182–2431. Jacket required. AE, DC, MC, V.*

$$$$ ✕ **V Zátiší.** White walls and casual grace accentuate the sub-
★ tle flavors of smoked salmon, plaice, beef Wellington, and other non-Czech specialties. Order the house *Rulandské červené*, a fruity Moravian red wine that meets the exacting standards of the food. In behavior unusual for the city, the benign waiters fairly fall over each other to serve diners. ⊠ *Liliová 1, Betlémské nám., Staré Město,* ☏ *02/2422–8977. AE, DC, MC, V.*

$$$ ✕ **Fakhreldine.** This elegant Lebanese restaurant, crowded with diplomats who know where to find the real thing, has an excellent range of Middle Eastern appetizers and main courses. For a moderately priced meal, try several appetizers—hummus and garlic yogurt, perhaps—instead of a main course. ⊠ *Klimentská 48, Prague 1,* ☏ *02/232–7970. AE, DC, MC, V.*

$$ ✕ **U Rychtáře** (The Landlord's). A contender for best Italian restaurant in Prague, there's plenty to tempt here, from 20 pasta dishes to nine pizzas, fish courses, and flavorful omelets. Especially tasty are the linguine with chicken breast, ginger, shallots, and parsley and farfalle with broccoli and pepper sauce. The classic Italian desserts, *tiramisù* and *tartuffo*, are crafted with love. ⊠ *Dlouhá 2, Prague 1,* ☏ *02/232–7207. AE, MC, DC, V.*

$ ✕ **Kogo Pizzeria-Caffeteria.** This is an appealing, laid-back place that serves divine cappuccino and reasonably priced Italian food with hints of Mediterranean fare. Recommended are blue-cheese pasta, and Kogo pizza (ham, peppers, basil, and Niva cheese). ⊠ *Havelská 27, Prague 1, no phone. No credit cards.*

$ ✕ **Profit.** The unfortunate name masks a clean, spacious pub that serves such excellent Czech standbys as goulash and pork with dumplings and sauerkraut at astonishingly reasonable prices. The central location could hardly be better. ⊠ *Betlémské nám. 8, Staré Město,* ☏ *02/2422–2776. No credit cards.*

Prague Dining

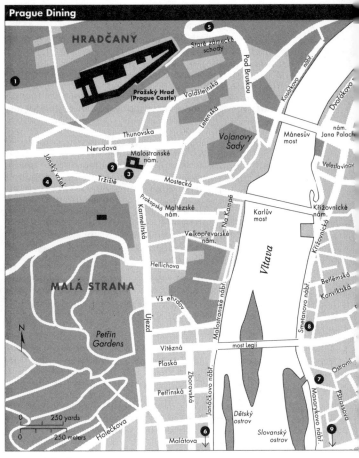

Bella Napoli, **14**	Penguin's, **6**	U Mecenáše, **2**
Cerberus, **23**	Pezinok, **12**	U Počtů, **5**
Dolly Bell, **9**	Pizzeria Coloseum, **13**	U Rychtáře, **20**
Fakhreldine, **22**	Potomac, **21**	U Tři Zlatých Hvězd, **3**
Kogo Pizzeria-Caffeteria, **19**	Profit, **11**	U Zlaté Hrušky, **1**
Lobkovická, **4**	Rusalka, **7**	V Krakovské, **15**
Myslivna, **18**	Taj Mahal, **17**	V Zátiší, **10**
Na Zvonařce, **16**		
Parnas, **8**		

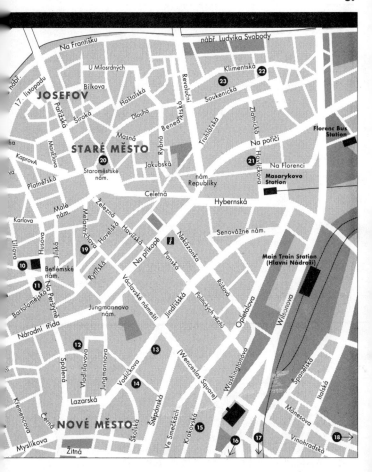

New Town (Nové Město)

$$$$ ✕ **Parnas.** The first choice for visiting dignitaries and businesspeople blessed with expense accounts, Parnas has creative, freshly prepared cuisine, more nouvelle than Bohemian, served in an opulent 1920s setting. Window seats afford stunning views of Prague Castle. There is a small, mostly Czech vintage wine list and a fine selection of appetizers and desserts (the chocolate mousse is a must). ⊠ *Smetanovo nábřeží 2, Nové Město,* ☎ *02/2422–7614. Jacket required. AE, DC, MC, V.*

$$$$ ✕ **Taj Mahal.** Authentic Indian food in Prague? It's not as far-fetched as it once was. Specialties of northern and southern India are the focus at Taj Mahal, and the tandoori chicken is divine. ⊠ *Krétova 10, Prague 1 (near metro Muzeum),* ☎ *02/2422–5566. AE, MC, V.*

$$$ ✕ **Cerberus.** Traditional Czech cooking is raised to an uncommonly high level at this New Town restaurant. The Bohemian staples of pork, duck, rabbit, and game are prepared and presented (by an attentive staff) as haute cuisine. Despite the modern decor, the ambience is warm and intimate. ⊠ *Soukenická 19, Nové Město,* ☎ *02/231–0985. AE, MC, V.*

$$ ✕ **Bella Napoli.**
★ Come here for real Italian food at a price-to-quality ratio that's hard to beat in Prague. Ignore the faux Italian interior and the alabaster Venus de Milos astride shopping-mall fountains and head straight for the 65 Kč antipasto bar, which will distract you with fresh olives, eggplant, squid, and mozzarella. For your main course, go with any of a dozen superb pasta dishes or splurge with shrimp or chicken parmigiana. The Italian-American chef hails from Brooklyn and knows his stuff. ⊠ *V jámě 8, Nové Město,* ☎ *02/ 2422–7315. No credit cards.*

$$ ✕ **Dolly Bell.**
★ Whimsically designed, the upside-down tables hanging from the ceiling provide a clever counterpoint to the huge selection of Yugoslav dishes, with an emphasis on meat and seafood. Especially worth sampling are the cornbread with Balkan cheese, cheese pie, and meat-filled pastry. ⊠ *Neklanova 20, Prague 2,* ☎ *02/298–815. AE, DC, MC, V.*

$$ ✕ **Na Zvonařce.** This bright beer hall supplements traditional Czech dishes—mostly pork, beer, and more pork—with some innovative Czech and international choices, all at unbeatably cheap prices. Noteworthy entrées include juicy fried chicken and English roast beef; fruit dumplings for dessert are a rare treat. The service may be slow, but that simply allows time to commune with a tankard of ale on the outside terrace during the summer. ⊠ *Šafaříkova 1, Prague 2,* ☏ *02/691–1311. No credit cards.*

$$ ✕ **Pezinok.** Slovak cooking is hard to find in Prague, and this cozy wine restaurant is still the best in town. Heavy furnishings and subdued lighting add an oddly formal touch. Order à la carte (the set menus are overpriced) and choose from homemade sausages or *halušky*, boiled noodles served with tangy sheep's cheese. The restaurant's full-bodied wines come from the Slovak town for which the restaurant is named. ⊠ *Purkyňova 4, Nové Město,* ☏ *02/ 291996. AE, DC, MC, V.*

$$ ✕ **Rusalka.** This quiet, cozy nook is the perfect pre- or post-theater dining spot, named after Dvořák's beloved opera, and it's right behind the National Theater. International specialties are presented with flair: Try the spicy Japanese chicken soup and chicken in sage and farfalle. ⊠ *Na struze 1/277, Prague 1,* ☏ *02/2491–5876. AE, MC, V.*

$$ ✕ **V Krakovské.** At this clean, proper pub close to the major tourist sights, the food is traditional and hearty; this is the place to try Bohemian duck, washed down with a dark beer from Domažlice in western Bohemia. ⊠ *Krakovská 20, Nové Město,* ☏ *02/261–537. No credit cards.*

$ ✕ **Pizzeria Coloseum.** Delicious pizza to satisfy all tastes, and the location can't be beat: right off Wenceslas Square. The picnic tables makes this an ideal spot for an informal lunch or dinner. There's a salad bar, too. ⊠ *Vodiākova 32, Prague 1,* ☏ *02/2421–4914. AE, V.*

Malá Strana

$$$$ ✕ **U Mecenáše.** A fetching Renaissance inn from the 17th century, with dark, high-backed benches in the front room and cozy, elegant sofas and chairs in back, this is the place to splurge: From the aperitifs to the steaks and the cognac (swirled lovingly in oversize glasses), the presentation is seamless. ⊠ *Malostranské nám. 10, Malá Strana,* ☏ *02/533881. Jacket required. AE, DC, MC, V.*

$$$ ✕ **Lobkovická.** This dignified *vinárna* (wine hall) set inside
★ a 17th-century town palace serves some of Prague's most imaginative dishes. Chicken breast with crabmeat and curry

sauce is an excellent main dish and typical of the kitchen's innovative approach to sauces and spices. Deep-red carpeting sets the perfect mood for enjoying bottles of Moravian wine brought from the musty depths of the restaurant's wine cellar. ✉ *Vlašská 17, Malá Strana,* ☎ *02/530185. Jacket and tie. AE, DC, MC, V.*

$$ ✕ **U Tří Zlatých Hvězd** (the Three Golden Stars). A perfect spot for a romantic evening, the cuisine is hearty, classic Czech with thoughtful European touches. Recommended are rose of smoked salmon with dill mayonnaise as a starter, followed by roast duck Bohemian style with apples, bacon, dumplings, and red cabbage. ✉ *Malostranské nám. 8, Prague 1,* ☎ FAX *02/539660. AE, DC, MC, V.*

Hradčany

$$$$ ✕ **U Zlaté Hrušky.** At this bustling bistro perched on one of Prague's prettiest cobblestone streets, slide into one of the cozy dark-wood booths and let the cheerful staff advise on wines and specials. Duck and carp are house favorites. After dinner, stroll to the castle for an unforgettable panorama. ✉ *Nový Svět 3, Hradčany,* ☎ *02/531133. Jacket and tie. AE, DC, MC, V.*

Vinohrady

$$ ✕ **Myslivna.** The name means "hunting lodge," and the cooks at this far-flung neighborhood eatery certainly know their way around venison, quail, and boar. Attentive staff can advise on wines: Try Vavřinecké, a hearty red that holds its own with any beast. The stuffed quail and the leg of venison with walnuts both get high marks. A cab from the city center to Myslivna should cost under 200 Kč. ✉ *Jagellonska 21, Prague 3,* ☎ *02/6270209. AE, V.*

Letná, Holešovice

$$ ✕ **U Počtů.** Superior, discreet service, a relative rarity in Prague, heightens the pleasure of dining at this charmingly old-fashioned restaurant. Midnight garlic soup and chicken livers in wine sauce are flawlessly rendered, and grilled trout is delicious. ✉ *Milády Horakové 47, Prague 7,* ☎ *02/370085. MC, V.*

Smíchov

$$ ✕ **Penguin's.** The emphasis at this popular eatery is on classic Czech and international dishes, served in an elegant mauve-and-matte-black setting. Try any of the steaks or the chicken breast with potatoes. The penguin in the name refers to the Pittsburgh variety, of hockey fame—the owner's favorite team. ✉ *Zborovská 5, Prague 5,* ☎ *02/545660. No credit cards.*

4 Lodging

Lodging

VISITORS are frequently disappointed by the city's lodging options. Hotel owners were quick to raise prices after 1989, when tourists first began flocking to Prague, but they have been much, much slower in raising their facilities to Western standards. In most of the $$$$ and $$$ hotels, you can expect to find a restaurant and an exchange bureau on or near the premises. Bills are paid in Czech crowns, though some hotels still insist you pay in hard (that is, Western) currency; be certain to inquire *before* making a reservation. During the summer season reservations are absolutely imperative; the remainder of the year they are highly recommended.

A cheaper and often more interesting alternative to Prague's generally mediocre hotels are private rooms and apartments. Prague is full of travel agencies offering such accommodations; sacrificing a little privacy is the only drawback. The biggest room-finding service is probably **AVE** (☎ 02/2422–3226, FAX 02/549744), with offices in the main train station (✉ Hlavní nádraží) and at Holešovice station (✉ Nádraží Holešovice). Both offices are open daily from 7 AM to 10 PM. Their Ruzyně Airport office is open from 7 AM to 9 PM. Prices start at around $15 per person per night. Insist on a room in the city center, however, or you may find yourself in a dreary, far-flung suburb. Other helpful room-finding agencies include **Hello Ltd.** (✉ Senovážné nám. 3, Nové Město, ☎ FAX 02/2421–2741) and **City of Prague Accommodation Service** (✉ Haštalské nám. 8, Staré Město, ☎ 02/231–0202, FAX 02/2481–0603), which is open daily 8–8, until 10 in summer. Čedok and Prague Information Service (PIS) offices can also help in locating private accommodations. If all else fails, just take a walk through the Old Town: The number of places advertising ACCOMMODATION (often written in German as UNTERKUNFT) is astounding.

CATEGORY	PRICE*
$$$$	over $200
$$$	$100–$200
$$	$50–$100
$	under $50

All prices are for a standard double room during peak season.

$$$$ ★ **Diplomat.** This sprawling complex opened in 1990 and remains one of the best business hotels in town. Even though it's in the suburbs, the Diplomat is convenient to the airport and, via the metro, to the city center. The modern rooms may not exude much character, but they are tastefully furnished and quite comfortable. Hotel staff members are competent and many are bilingual. Guests have access to a pool, sauna, and fitness center. ✉ *Evropská 15, 160 00 Prague 6,* ☎ *02/2439–4111,* FAX *02/2439–4215. 387 rooms with bath. 2 restaurants, bar, pool, sauna, health club, nightclub, conference room. AE, DC, MC, V.*

$$$$ **Grand Hotel Bohemia.** This beautifully refurbished art-nouveau town palace is just a stone's throw from the Old Town Square. The Austrian owners opted for a muted, modern decor in the rooms but left the sumptuous public areas just as they were. Each room is outfitted with a fax and answering machine. ✉ *Králodvorska 4, 110 00 Prague 1,* ☎ *02/2480–4111,* FAX *02/232–9545. 78 rooms with bath. Restaurant, café. AE, DC, MC, V.*

$$$$ **Palace.** For the well-heeled, this is Prague's most coveted address—an art-nouveau town palace perched on a busy corner only a block from the very central Wenceslas Square. Renovated in 1989, the hotel's spacious, well-appointed rooms, each with a private white-marble bathroom, are fitted in velvety pinks and greens cribbed straight from an Alfons Mucha print. Two rooms are set aside for travelers with disabilities. The ground-floor buffet boasts the city's finest salad bar. ✉ *Panská 12, 110 00 Prague 1,* ☎ *02/2409–3111,* FAX *02/2422–1240. 125 rooms with bath. 2 restaurants, bar, café, snack bar, satellite TV, minibars, sauna. AE, DC, MC, V.*

$$$$ **U Tří Pštrosů.** The location could not be better—a romantic corner in the Malá Strana only a stone's throw from the river and within arms' reach of the Charles Bridge. The airy rooms, dating back 300 years, still have their original oak-beamed ceilings and antique furniture; many also have views over the river. Massive walls keep out the noise of the crowds on the bridge. An excellent in-house restaurant serves traditional Czech dishes to guests and nonguests alike. ✉ *Dražického nám. 12, 118 00 Prague 1,* ☎ *02/2451–0779,* FAX *02/2451–0783. 18 rooms with bath. Restaurant. AE, MC, V (no credit cards in restaurant).*

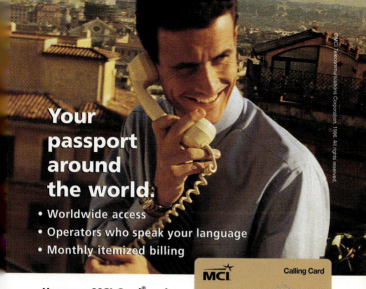

Your passport around the world.

- Worldwide access
- Operators who speak your language
- Monthly itemized billing

Use your MCI Card® and these access numbers for an easy way to call when traveling worldwide.

Austria (CC)♦†	022-903-012
Belarus	
From Gomel and Mogilev regions	8-10-800-103
From all other localities	8-800-103
Belgium (CC)♦†	0800-10012
Bulgaria	00800-0001
Croatia (CC)★	99-385-0112
Czech Republic (CC)♦	00-42-000112
Denmark (CC)♦†	8001-0222
Finland (CC)♦†	9800-102-80
France (CC)♦†	0800-99-0019
Germany (CC)†	0130-0012
Greece (CC)♦†	00-800-1211
Hungary (CC)♦	00▼800-01411
Iceland (CC)♦†	800-9002
Ireland (CC)†	1-800-55-1001
Italy (CC)♦†	172-1022
Kazakhstan (CC)	1-800-131-4321
Liechtenstein (CC)♦	155-0222
Luxembourg†	0800-0112
Monaco (CC)♦	800-90-19
Netherlands (CC)♦†	06-022-91-22
Norway (CC)♦†	800-19912
Poland (CC)✥†	00-800-111-21-22
Portugal (CC)✥†	05-017-1234
Romania (CC)✥	01-800-1800
Russia (CC)✥♦	747-3322
For a Russian-speaking operator	747-3320
San Marino (CC)♦	172-1022
Slovak Republic (CC)	00-42-000112
Slovenia	080-8808
Spain (CC)†	900-99-0014
Sweden (CC)♦†	020-795-922
Switzerland (CC)♦†	155-0222
Turkey (CC)♦†	00-8001-1177
Ukraine (CC)✥	8▼10-013
United Kingdom (CC)†	
To call to the U.S. using BT■	0800-89-0222
To call to the U.S. using Mercury■	0500-89-0222
Vatican City (CC)†	172-1022

To sign up for the MCI Card, dial the access number of the country you are in and ask to speak with a customer service representative.

http://www.mci.com

(CC) Country-to-country calling available. May not be available to/from all international locations. (Canada, Puerto Rico, and U.S. Virgin Islands are considered Domestic Access locations.) ♦ Public phones may require deposit of coin or phone card for dial tone. † Automation available from most locations. ★ Not available from public pay phones. ▼ Wait for second dial tone. ✥ Limited availability. ■ International communications carrier.

It helps to be pushy in airports.

Introducing the revolutionary new TransPorter™ from American Tourister.® It's the first suitcase you can push around without a fight. TransPorter's™ exclusive four-wheel design lets you push it in front of you with almost no effort–the wheels take the weight. Or pull it on two wheels if you choose. You can even stack on other bags and use it like a luggage cart. TransPorter™ is designed like a dresser, with built-in shelves to organize your belongings. Or collapse the shelves and pack it like a traditional suitcase. Inside, there's a suiter feature to help keep suits and dresses from wrinkling. When push comes to shove, you can't beat a TransPorter.™ For more information on how you can be this pushy, call 1-800-542-1300.

Stable 4-wheel design.

Shelves collapse on command.

Making travel less primitive.®

©1996 American Tourister®

Lodging

$$$ **Axa.** Funky and functional, this modernist high-rise, built in 1932, was a mainstay of the budget-hotel crowd until a makeover forced substantial price hikes. The rooms, now with color television sets and modern plumbing, are certainly improved; however, the lobby and public areas look decidedly tacky, with plastic flowers and glaring lights. ✉ *Na poříčí 40, 113 03 Prague 1,* ☎ *02/2481–2580,* FAX *02/2481–2067. 109 rooms, most with bath. Restaurant, bar, pool, exercise room, nightclub. AE, DC, MC, V.*

$$$ **City Hotel Moráň.** This 19th-century town house was tastefully renovated in 1992; now the lobby and public areas are bright and inviting, made over in an updated Jugendstil style. The modern if slightly bland rooms are a cut above the Prague standard for convenience and cleanliness; ask for one on the sixth floor for a good view of Prague Castle. ✉ *Na Moráni 15, 120 00 Prague 2 (corner of Václavská),* ☎ *02/2491–5208,* FAX *02/297533. 53 rooms, most with bath. Restaurant, bar. AE, DC, MC, V.*

$$$ **Harmony.** This is one of the newly renovated, formerly state-owned standbys. The stern 1930s facade clashes with the bright, nouveau riche–type 1990s interior, but cheerful receptionists and big, clean rooms compensate for the aesthetic flaws. Ask for a room away from the bustle of one of Prague's busiest streets. ✉ *Na poříčí 31, 110 00 Prague 1,* ☎ *02/232–0720,* FAX *02/231–0009. 60 rooms with bath. Restaurant, snack bar. AE, DC, MC, V.*

$$$ **Kampa.** This early baroque armory turned hotel is
★ tucked away on a leafy corner at the southern end of Malá Strana. The rooms are clean, if sparse, though the bucolic setting makes up for any discomforts. Note the late-Gothic vaulting in the massive dining room. ✉ *Všehrdova 16, 118 00 Prague 1,* ☎ *02/2451–0409,* FAX *02/2451–0377. 85 rooms with bath. Restaurant, café. AE, DC, MC, V.*

$$$ **Meteor Plaza.** This popular Old Town hotel, operated by the Best Western chain, combines the best of New World convenience and Old World charm (Empress Maria Theresa's son, Joseph, stayed here when he was passing through in the 18th century). The setting is ideal: a renovated baroque building that is only five minutes on foot from downtown. There is a good, if touristy, in-house wine cellar. ✉ *Hybernská 6, 110 00 Prague 1,* ☎ *02/2422–0664,* FAX

Prague Lodging

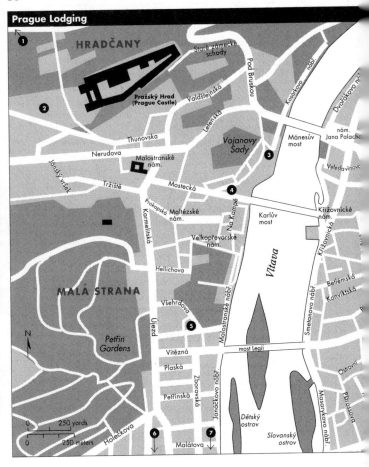

Apollo, **18**
Astra, **10**
Axa, **14**
Balkan, **7**
City Hotel Moráň, **9**
Diplomat, **1**
Grand Hotel Bohemia, **13**
Harmony, **15**
Kampa, **5**
Mepro, **6**
Meteor Plaza, **12**
Opera, **16**
Palace, **11**
Pension Louda, **17**
Pension U raka, **2**
Pension Unitas, **8**
U páva, **3**
U tří pštrosů, **4**

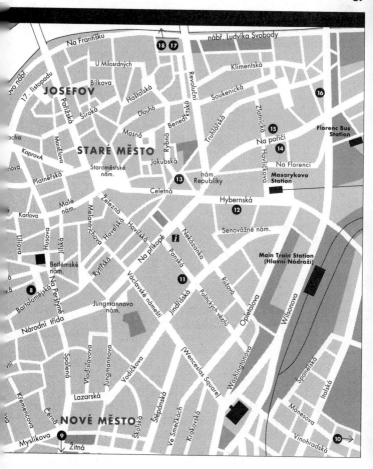

02/2421–3005. *86 rooms with bath. Restaurant, business center. AE, DC, MC, V.*

$$$ ★ **Pension U Raka.** This private guest house offers the peace and coziness of an alpine lodge, plus a quiet location on the ancient, winding streets of Nový Svět, just behind the Loreto Church and a 10-minute walk from Prague Castle. The dark-wood building has only five rooms, but if you can get a reservation (try at least a month in advance), you will gain a wonderful base for exploring Prague. ⊠ *Černínská ul. 10/93, 118 00 Prague 1,* ☎ *02/351453 or 02/2051–1100,* FAX *02/353074 or 02/2051–0511. 5 rooms. AE, DC, MC, V.*

$$$ ★ **U Páva.** This neoclassical inn, on a quiet gaslit street in Malá Strana, offers upstairs suites that afford an unforgettable view of Prague Castle. Best of all, the U Páva is small and intimate—the perfect escape for those who've had their fill of cement high-rise resorts. The staff is courteous and helpful, while the reception and public areas are elegant and discreet. ⊠ *U lužického semináře 32, 118 00 Prague 1,* ☎ *02/2451–0922,* FAX *02/533379. 11 rooms with bath. Restaurant, bar. AE, DC, MC, V.*

$$ **Apollo.** This is a standard, no-frills, square-box hotel where clean rooms come at a fair price. Its primary flaw is its location: roughly 20 minutes by metro or bus from the city center. ⊠ *Kubišova 23, 182 00 Prague 8 (metro Holešovice, Line C, then Tram 5, 17, or 25 to the Hercovka stop),* ☎ *02/688–0628,* FAX *02/688–4570. 35 rooms with bath. AE, MC, V.*

$$ **Astra.** The location best serves drivers coming in to town from the east, although the nearby metro station makes this modern hotel easy to reach from the center. It's good value at the price. ⊠ *Mukařovská 1740/18, 100 00 Prague 10 (from metro station Skalka, Line A, walk south on Na padesátém about 5 mins to Mukařovská),* ☎ *02/781–3595,* FAX *02/781–0765. 50 rooms with bath. Restaurant, in-room satellite TVs, nightclub. AE, DC, MC, V.*

$$ **Mepro.** Standard rooms and service and a reasonably central location make this small hotel worth considering. The Smíchov neighborhood offers a good range of restaurants (for one, the U Mikuláše Dačického wine tavern, across the street from the hotel) and nice strolls along the river or up the Petřín hill. ⊠ *Viktora Huga 3, 150 00 Prague 5,* ☎ *02/*

549167, FAX 02/561–8587. *26 rooms with bath. Snack bar, in-room satellite TVs. AE, MC, V.*

$$ ⛨ **Opera.** Once the lodging of choice for divas performing at the nearby State Theater, the Opera greatly declined under the Communists. New owners, however, are working hard to restore the hotel's former luster. Until then, the clean (but smallish) rooms, friendly staff, and fin de siècle charm are still reason enough to recommend it. Rooms without bath are half price. ✉ *Těšnov 13, 110 00 Prague 1,* ☎ *02/231–5609,* FAX *02/231–1477. 66 rooms, some with bath. Restaurant, bar. AE, DC, MC, V.*

$ ⛨ **Balkan.** One of the few central hotels that can compete in cost with private rooms, the spartan Balkan is on a busy street, not far from Malá Strana and the National Theater. ✉ *Svornosti 28, 150 00 Prague 5,* ☎ FAX *02/540777. 24 rooms with bath. Breakfast not included. Restaurant. AE.*

$ ⛨ **Pension Louda.** The friendly owners of this family-run
★ guest house, set in a suburb roughly 20 minutes by tram from the city center, go out of their way to make you feel welcome. The large, spotless rooms are an unbelievable bargain, and the hilltop location offers a stunning view of greater Prague. ✉ *Kubišova 10, 182 00 Prague 8 (metro Holešovice, Line C, then Tram 5, 17, or 25 to the Hercovka stop),* ☎ *02/688–1491,* FAX *02/688–1488. 9 rooms with bath. No credit cards.*

$ ⛨ **Pension Unitas.** Operated by the Christian charity Unitas in an Old Town convent, the spartan rooms at this well-run establishment used to serve as interrogation cells for the Communist secret police. Conditions are much more comfortable nowadays, if far from luxurious. Alcohol and tobacco are not permitted. ✉ *Bartolomějská 9, 110 00 Prague 1,* ☎ *02/232–7700,* FAX *02/232–7709. 40 rooms, none with bath. AE, MC, V.*

5 Nightlife and the Arts

NIGHTLIFE

Cabaret
For adult stage entertainment (with some nudity) try the **Lucerna Bar** (⊠ Štěpánská ul. 61, at Wenceslas Sq.) or **Varieté Praga** (⊠ Vodičkova ul. 30, ☎ 02/2421–5945).

Discos
Dance clubs come and go with predictable regularity. The longtime favorite is **Radost FX** (⊠ Bělehradská 120, Prague 2, ☎ 02/251210), featuring imported DJs playing the latest dance music and techno from London. The café on the ground floor is open all night and serves wholesome vegetarian food. Two popular discos for dancing the night away with fellow tourists are **Lávká** (⊠ Novotného lávká 1, near the Charles Bridge), featuring open-air dancing by the bridge on summer nights, and the **Corona Club and Latin Café** (⊠ Novotného lávká, Prague 1), which highlights Latin, Gypsy and other dance-friendly live music. Discos catering to a very young crowd blast sound onto lower Wenceslas Square.

Jazz Clubs
Jazz gained notoriety under the Communists as a subtle form of protest, and the city still has some great jazz clubs, featuring everything from swing to blues and modern. **Reduta** (⊠ Národní 20, ☎ 02/2491–2246) features a full program of local and international musicians. **AghaRTA** (⊠ Krakovská 5, ☎ 02/2421–2914) offers a variety of jazz acts in an intimate café/nightclub atmosphere. Music starts around 9 PM, but come earlier to get a seat. Check posters around town or any of the English-language newspapers for current listings.

Pubs, Bars, and Lounges
Bars or lounges are not traditional Prague fixtures; social life, of the drinking variety, usually takes place in pubs (*pivnice* or *hospody*), which are liberally sprinkled throughout the city's neighborhoods. Tourists are welcome to join in the evening ritual of sitting around large tables and talking, smoking, and drinking beer. Before venturing in, however, it's best to familiarize yourself with a few points of pub etiquette: Always ask if a chair is free before sitting down. To order a beer (*pivo*), do not wave the waiter down

or shout across the room; he will usually assume you want beer and bring it over to you without asking. He will also bring subsequent rounds to the table without asking. To refuse, just shake your head or say no thanks. At the end of the evening, usually around 10:30 or 11:00, the waiter will come to tally the bill. Some of the most popular pubs in the city center include **U Medvídků** (✉ Na Perštýně 7), **U Vejvodů** (✉ Jilská 4), and **U Zlatého Tygra** (✉ Husova ul. 17). All can get impossibly crowded.

One of the oddest phenomena of Prague's post-1989 renaissance is the sight of travelers and tour groups from the United States, Britain, Australia, and even Japan descending on this city to experience the life of—American expatriates. There are a handful of bars guaranteed to ooze Yanks and other native English speakers. **Jo's Bar** (✉ Malostranské nám. 7) is a haven for younger expats, serving bottled beer, mixed drinks, and good Mexican food. The **James Joyce Pub** (✉ Liliová 10) is authentically Irish, with Guinness on tap and excellent food. **U Malého Glena** puts on live jazz, folk, and rock (✉ Karmelitská 23, ☎ 02/535–8115). The major hotels also run their own bars and nightclubs. The **Piano Bar** (✉ Hotel Palace, Panská ul. 12) is the most pleasant of the lot; jacket and tie are suggested.

Rock Clubs

Prague's rock scene is thriving. Hard-rock enthusiasts should check out the **Rock Café** (✉ Národní 20, ☎ 02/2491–4416) or **Strahov 007** (✉ Near Strahov Stadium; take Bus 218 2 stops from Anděl metro station). **RC Bunkr** (✉ Lodecká 2, ☎ 02/2481–0665) was the first postrevolutionary underground club. The **Malostranska Beseda** (✉ Malostranské nám. 21, ☎ 02/539024) and the **Belmondo Revival Club** (✉ Bubenská 1, Prague 7, ☎ 02/791–4854) are dependable bets for sometimes bizarre, but always good, musical acts from around the country.

THE ARTS

Prague's cultural flair is legendary, though performances are usually booked far in advance by all sorts of Praguers. The concierge at your hotel may be able to reserve tickets for you. Otherwise, for the cheapest tickets go directly to

The Arts

the theater box office a few days in advance or immediately before a performance. The biggest ticket agency, **Tiketpro,** has outlets all over town and accepts credit cards (main branch at ⊠ Štěpánská 61, Lucerna passage, ☏ 02/2481–4020). **Bohemia Ticket International** (⊠ Na příkopě 16, ☏ 02/2421–5031; ⊠ Václavské nám. 25, ☏ 02/2422–7253) sells tickets for major cultural events, though at semi-inflated prices. Tickets can also be purchased at **American Express** (⊠ Václavské nám. 56).

For details of cultural events, look for the English-language newspaper the *Prague Post* or the monthly *Velvet* magazine, or the monthly *Prague Guide,* available at hotels and tourist offices.

Film

If a film was made in the United States or Britain, the chances are good that it will be shown with Czech subtitles rather than dubbed. (Film titles, however, are usually translated into Czech, so your only clue to the movie's country of origin may be the poster used in advertisements.) Popular cinemas are **Blaník** (⊠ Václavské nám. 56, ☏ 02/2421–6698), **Hvěda** (⊠ Václavské nám 38, ☏ 02/264545), **Praha** (⊠ Václavské nám. 17, ☏ 02/262035), and **Světozor** (⊠ Vodičkova ul. 39, ☏ 02/263616). Prague's English-language publications carry film reviews and full timetables.

Music

Classical concerts are held all over the city throughout the year. The best orchestral venues are the resplendent art-nouveau **Obecní dům** (⊠ Smetana Hall, Nám. Republiky 5, scheduled to reopen in the spring of 1997), home of the Prague Symphony Orchestra, and **Dvořák Hall** (⊠ In the Rudolfinum, nám. Jana Palacha, ☏ 02/2489–3111). The latter concert hall is home to one of Central Europe's best orchestras, the Czech Philharmonic, which has been racked in recent years by bitter disputes among players, conductors, and management but still plays sublimely.

Performances also are held regularly in the **Garden on the Ramparts** below Prague Castle (where the music comes with a view), the two **churches of St. Nicholas** (on Old Town Square and Malostranské náměstí), the **Church of Sts. Simon** and Jude (⌧ Dušní ul., in the Old Town, near the Hotel Inter-Continental), the **Church of St. James** (⌧ Malá Štupartská, near Old Town Square), the **Zrcadlová kaple** (⌧ Mirror Chapel, Klementinum, Mariánské náměstí, Old Town), the **Lobkowicz Palace** at Prague Castle, and plenty more palaces and churches. Dozens of classical ensembles survive off the tourist-concert trade at these and many other venues. The standard of performance ranges from adequate to superb, though the programs tend to take few risks. Serious fans of baroque music have the opportunity to hear works of little-known Bohemian composers at these concerts. Some of the best chamber ensembles are the **Talich Chamber Orchestra,** the **Guarneri Trio,** the **Wihan Quartet,** the **Czech Piano Trio,** and the **Agon** contemporary music group.

Concerts at the **Villa Bertramka** (⌧ Mozartova 169, Smíchov, ☎ 02/543893) emphasize the music of Mozart and his contemporaries.

Fans of organ music will be delighted by the number of recitals held in Prague's historic halls and churches. Popular programs are offered at **St. Vitus Cathedral** in Hradčany, **U Křížovníků** near the Charles Bridge, the **Church of St. Nicholas** in Malá Strana, and **St. James's Church** on Malá Štupartská in the Old Town, where the organ plays amid a complement of baroque statuary.

Opera and Ballet

The Czech Republic has a strong operatic tradition, and performances at the **Národní divadlo** (⌧ National Theater, Národní třída 2, ☎ 02/2491–2673) and the **Statní Opera Praha** (⌧ State Opera House, Wilsonova 4, ☎ 02/265353), near the top of Wenceslas Square, can be excellent. It's always worthwhile to buy a cheap ticket (for as little as 10 Kč) just to take a look at these stunning 19th-century halls; appropriate attire is recommended. Now, unlike the Communist period, operas are almost always sung in their original tongue, and the repertoire offers plenty of Italian favorites and the Czech national composers Janaček, Dvořák, and Smetana. The historic **Stavovské divadlo** (⌧ Estates' Theater, Ovocný trh. 1, ☎ 02/2421–5001), where *Don Giovanni* premiered in the 18th century, plays host to a mix of operas and dramatic works. Simultaneous translation into English via a microwave transmitter and headsets is usually offered at drama performances. The National and State theaters also occasionally have ballets.

Puppet Shows

This traditional form of Czech popular entertainment has been given new life thanks to the productions mounted at the **National Marionette Theater** (⊠ Žatecká 1) and the **Magic Theater of the Baroque World** (⊠ Celetná 13). Traditionally, children and adults alike enjoy the hilarity and pathos of these performances.

Theater

Theater thrives in the Czech Republic as a vibrant art form. A dozen or so professional companies play in Prague to ever-packed houses; the language barrier can't obscure the players' artistry. Tourist-friendly, nonverbal theater abounds as well, notably Black Theater, a melding of live acting, mime, video, and stage trickery, which continues to draw crowds despite signs of fatigue. The famous **Laterna Magika** (Magic Lantern) puts on a similar extravaganza (⊠ Národní třída 4, ☎ 02/2491–4129). Performances usually begin at 7 or 7:30 PM. Several English-language theater groups operate sporadically in Prague; pick up a copy of the *Prague Post* for complete listings.

6 Shopping

DESPITE THE RELATIVE SHORTAGE of quality clothes—Prague has a long way to go before it can match shopping meccas Paris and Rome—the capital is a great place to pick up gifts and souvenirs. Bohemian crystal and porcelain deservedly enjoy a worldwide reputation for quality, and plenty of shops offer excellent bargains. The local market for antiques and artwork is still relatively undeveloped, while dozens of antiquarian bookstores can yield some excellent finds, particularly German and Czech books and graphics. Another bargain is recorded music: CD prices are about half what you would pay in the West.

Shopping Districts

The major shopping areas are **Národní třída,** running past Můstek to Na příkopě, and the area around **Staroměstské náměstí** (Old Town Square). **Pařížská ulice, Karlova ulice** (on the way to the Charles Bridge), and the area just south of **Josefov** (the Jewish Quarter) are also good places to find boutiques and antiques shops. In the Malá Strana, try **Nerudova ulice,** the street that runs up to the Castle Hill district.

Department Stores

These are not always well stocked and often have everything except the one item you're looking for, but a stroll through one may yield some interesting finds and bargains. The best are **Kotva** (⊠ Nám. Republiky 8), **Tesco** (⊠ Národní třída 26), **Bílá Labuť** (⊠ Na poříčí 23), and **Krone** (⊠ Václavské nám. 21).

Street Markets

For fruits and vegetables, the best street market in central Prague is on **Havelská ulice** in the Old Town. But arrive early in the day if you want something a bit more exotic than tomatoes and cucumbers. The best market for nonfood items is the flea market in **Holešovice,** north of the city center, although there isn't really much of interest here outside of cheap tobacco and electronics products. Take the metro Line C to the Vltavská station and then ride any tram heading east (running to the left as you exit the metro station). Exit at the first stop and follow the crowds.

Specialty Stores

ANTIQUES

Starožitnosti (antiques shops) are everywhere in Prague, but you'll need a sharp eye to distinguish truly valuable pieces from merely interesting ones. Many dealers carry old glassware and vases. Antique jewelry, many pieces featuring garnets, is also popular. Remember to retain your receipts as proof of legitimate purchases, otherwise you may have difficulty bringing antiques out of the country. Comparison shop at stores along Karlova ulice in the Old Town. Also check in and around the streets of the former Jewish ghetto for shops specializing in Jewish antiques and artifacts. **Art Program** (⊠ Nerudova ul. 28) in the Malá Strana has an especially beautiful collection of art-deco jewelry and glassware.

BOOKS AND PRINTS

It's hard to imagine a more beautiful bookstore than **U Karlova Mostu** (⊠ Karlova ul. 2, Staré Město, ☎ 02/2422–9205), with its impressive selection of old maps, prints, and rare books.

One shop that comes close in appeal to U Karlova Mostu is **Antikvariát Karel Křenek** (⊠ Celetná 31, ☎ 02/231–4734), near the Powder Tower in the Old Town. It stocks prints and graphics from the 1920s and '30s, in addition to a small collection of English books.

If you'd just like a good read, be sure to check out the **Globe Bookstore and Coffeehouse** (⊠ Janovského 14, Prague 7, ☎ 02/6671–2610), which is one of Prague's meccas for the local English-speaking community.

U Knihomola Bookstore and Café (⊠ Mánesova 79, Prague 2, ☎ 02/627–7770) is a close contender to the Globe for the best place to find the latest in English literature, plus it stocks the best selection of new English-language art books and guidebooks. It's near the metro stop Jiřího z Poděbrad.

CRYSTAL AND PORCELAIN

Moser (⊠ Na příkopě 12, ☎ 02/2421–1293), the flagship store for the world-famous Karlovy Vary glassmaker, is the first address for stylish, high-quality lead crystal and china. Even if you're not in the market to buy, stop by the store simply to browse through the elegant wood-paneled salesrooms on the second floor. The staff will gladly pack goods for traveling. **Bohemia** (✉ Pařížska 2, ☎ 02/2481–1023) carries a wide selection of porcelain from Karlovy Vary. If you still can not find anything, have no fear: There is a crystal shop on just about every street in central Prague.

FOOD

Specialty food stores have been slow to catch on in Prague. **Fruits de France** (✉ Jindřišská 9, Nové Město, ☎ 02/2422–0304) stocks Prague's freshest fruits and vegetables imported directly from France at Western prices. The bakeries at the **Krone** and **Kotva** department stores sell surprisingly delicious breads and pastries. Both stores also have large, well-stocked basement grocery stores.

FUN THINGS FOR CHILDREN

Children enjoy the beautiful watercolor and colored-chalk sets available in nearly every stationery store at rock-bottom prices. The Czechs are also master illustrators, and the books they've made for young "pre-readers" are some of the world's loveliest. Many stores also offer unique wooden toys, sure to delight any young child. For these, look in at **Obchod Vším Možným** (✉ Nerudova 45, ☎ 02/536941). For older children and teens, it's worth considering a Czech or Eastern European watch, telescope, or set of binoculars. The quality/price ratio is unbeatable.

JEWELRY

The **Granát** shop at Dlouhá 30 in the Old Town has a comprehensive selection of garnet jewelry, plus contemporary and traditional pieces set in gold and silver. Several shops specializing in gold jewelry line Wenceslas Square.

MUSICAL INSTRUMENTS

Melodia (✉ Jungmannova nám. 17, ☎ 02/2422–2500) carries a complete range of quality musical instruments at reasonable prices. **Capriccio** (✉ Újezd 15, Prague 1, ☎ 02/532507) is a great place to find sheet music of all kinds.

SPORTS EQUIPMENT

Adidas has an outlet at Na Příkopě 8. Department stores also sometimes carry medium-quality sports equipment.

CZECH VOCABULARY

Basics

English	Czech	Pronunciation
Please.	Prosím.	**pro**-seem
Thank you.	Děkuji.	**dyek**-oo-yee
Thank you very much.	Děkuji pěkně.	**dyek**-oo-yee **pyek**-nyeh
You're welcome (it's nothing).	Není zač.	neh-nee **zahtch**
Yes, thank you.	Ano, děkuji.	**ah**-no **dyek**-oo-yee
Nice to meet you.	Těší mě.	**tye**-shee myeh
Pardon me.	Pardon.	**par**-don
Pardon me (formal)	Promiňte.	**pro**-meen-teh
I'm sorry.	Je mi líto.	yeh mee **lee**-to
I don't understand.	Nerozumím.	**neh**-rohz-oom-eem
I don't speak Czech very well.	Mluvim česky jen trochu.	**mloo**-vim **ches**-ky yen **tro**-khoo
Do you speak English?	Mluvíte anglicky?	**mloo**-vit-eh ahng-**glit**-ski
Yes/No	Ano/ne	**ah**-no/neh
Speak slowly, please.	Mluvte pomalu, prosím.	**mloov**-teh poh-**mah**-lo **pro**-seem
Repeat, please.	Opakujte, prosím.	**oh**-pahk-ooey-teh **pro**-seem
I don't know.	Nevím.	**neh**-veem

Questions

What . . . What is this?	Co . . . Co je to?	**tso** yeh toh
When . . . When will it be ready?	Kdy . . . Kdy to bude hotové?	g'**dih** toh **boo**-deh **hoh**-toh-veh
Who . . . Who is your friend?	Kdo . . . Kdo je váš přítel?	g'**doh** yeh vahsh **pshee**-tel
How . . . How do you say this in Czech?	Jak . . . Jak se to řekne česky?	yak seh toh **zhek**-neh **ches**-kee

This material is adapted from the Living Language™ *Fast & Easy series (Crown Publishers, Inc.). Fast & Easy "survival" courses are available in 15 different languages, including Czech, Hungarian, Polish, and Russian. Each interactive 60-minute cassette teaches more than 300 essential phrases for travelers. Available in bookstores, or call 800/733–3000 to order.*

Czech Vocabulary

Which . . . Which train goes to Bratislava?	Který . . . Který vlak jede do Bratislavy?	k'**tair**-ee vlahk **yeh**-deh doh **brat**islavee
What do you want to do?	Co chcete dělat?	tso kh'**tseh**-teh **dyeh**-laht
Where are you going?	Kam jdete?	kahm **dyeh**-teh
What is today's date?	Kolikátého je dnes?	**ko**-li-kah-**teh**-ho yeh d'nes
May I?/I'd like permission (to do something)	S dovolením, prosím.	s'**doh**-voh-leh-**neem pro**-seem
May I . . . ?	Smím . . . ?	smeem
May I take this?	Smím si to vžít?	**smeem** see toh v'**zheet**
May I enter?	Smím vstoupit?	smeem v'**sto**-pit
May I take a photo?	Smím fotografovat?	smeem **fo**-to-gra-fo-vaht

Numbers

Zero	Nula	**noo**-la
One	Jeden, jedna, jedno	ye-**den, yed**-nah, **yed**-no
Two	Dva, dvě	dvah, dvyeh
Three	Tři	tshree
Four	Čtyři	ch'**ti**-zhee
Five	Pět	pyet
Six	Šest	shest
Seven	Sedm	**sed**-oom
Eight	Osm	**oh**-soom
Nine	Devět	**deh**-vyet
Ten	Deset	**deh**-set
Eleven	Jedenáct	yeh-deh-**nahtst**
Twelve	Dvanáct	dvah-**nahtst**
Thirteen	Třináct	tshree-**nahtst**
Fourteen	Čtrnát	ch't'r-**nahtst**
Fifteen	Patnáct	paht-**nahtst**
Sixteen	Šestnáct	shest-**nahtst**
Seventeen	Sedmnáct	**sed**-oom-**nahtst**
Eighteen	Osmnáct	**oh**-soom-**nahtst**
Nineteen	Devatenáct	deh-**vah**-teh-**nahtst**
Twenty	Dvacet	**dvaht**-set
Twenty-one	Dvacet jedna	**dvaht**-set **yed**-nah
Twenty-two	Dvacet dva	**dvaht**-set dvah

Twenty-three	Dvacet tři	**dvaht**-set tshree
Thirty	Třicet	**tshree**-tset
Forty	Čtyřicet	ch**'ti**-zhee-tset
Fifty	Padesát	**pah**-deh-**saht**
Sixty	Šedesát	**sheh**-deh-saht
Seventy	Sedmdesát	**sed**-oom-deh-saht
Eighty	Osmdesát	**oh**-soom-deh-saht
Ninety	Devadesát	deh-**vah**-deh-saht
100	Sto	sto
1,000	Tisíc	**tee**-seets

Common Greetings

Hello/Good morning.	Dobrý den.	**dob**-ree den
Good evening.	Dobrý večer.	**dob**-ree **ve**-chair
Goodbye.	Na shledanou.	Na **sled**-ah-noh
Title for married woman (or unmarried older woman)	Paní	**pah**-nee
Title for young and unmarried woman	Slečno	**sletch**-noh
Title for man	Pan	**pan**
How do you do?	Jak se máte?	yak se **mah**-teh
Fine, thanks. And you?	Děkuji, dobře. A vy?	**dyek**-oo-yee **dobe**-zheh ah vee
What is your name?	Jak se jmenujete?	yak se **men**-weh-teh
My name is . . .	Jmenuji se . . .	**ymen**-weh-seh
I'll see you later.	Na shledanou brzo.	na **sled**-ah-noh **b'r**-zo
Good luck!	Mnoho štěstí!	m'**no**-ho **shtyes**-tee

Directions

Where is	Kde je	g'deh yeh
Excuse me. Where is the . . . ?	Promiňte, prosím. Kde je . . . ?	**pro**-meen-teh **pro**-seem g'deh yeh
Where is the bus stop?	Kde je autobusová zastávka?	g'deh yeh **ow**-to-boos-oh-vah zah-**stahv**-kah
Where is the subway station, please?	Kde je stanice metra, prosím?	g'deh je **stah**-nit-seh **meh**-trah **pro**-seem
Where is the rest room?	Kde jsou toalety, prosím?	g'deh so twa-**leh**-tee **pro**-seem

Czech Vocabulary

Go	Jděte	**dye**-teh
On the right	Napravo	**na**-pra-vo
On the left	Nalevo	**na**-leh-vo
Straight ahead	Rovně	**rohv**-nyeh
At (go to) the end of the street	Jděte na konec ulici	**dye**-teh na **ko**-nets **oo**-lit-si
The first left	První ulice nalevo	**per**-vnee **oo**-lit-seh **na**-leh-vo
Near	Blízko	**bleez**-ko
It's near here.	Je to blízko.	yeh to **bleez**-ko
Turn	Zahnete	**zah**-hneh-teh
Go back.	Jděte zpátky.	**dye**-teh z'**paht**-ky
Next to	Vedle	ved-**leh**

Shopping

Money	Peníze	pen-**ee**-zeh
Where is the bank?	Kde je banka?	g'deh yeh **bahn**-ka
I would like to change some money.	Chtěla bych si vyměnit peníze.	kh**'tyel**-ah bikh see vih-myen-it pen-**ee**-zeh
17 crowns	Sedmnáct korun	sed-oom-**nahtst** koh-**roon**
1,100 crowns	Tisíc sto korun	**tee**-seets sto koh-**roon**
3,000 crowns	Tři tisíce korun	tshree **tee**-see-tse koh-**roon**
Please write it down.	Napište to, prosím.	**nah**-peesh-tye toh **pro**-sim
What would you like?	Co si přejete?	tso see **pshay**-eh-teh
I would like this.	Chtěl bych tohle.	kh**'tyel** bikh **toh**-hleh
Here it is.	Tady to je.	**tah**-dee toh yeh
Is that all?	To je všechno?	toh yeh **vshekh**-no
Thanks, that's all.	Děkuji. To je všechno.	**dyek**-oo-yee toh yeh **vshekh**-no
Do you accept traveler's checks?	Přijímáte cestovni šeky?	**pshee**-yee-**mah**-teh **tses**-tohv-nee **shek**-ee
Credit cards?	Kredit Karty?	**cre**-dit **kar**-tee
How much?	Kolik?	**ko**-lik
Department store	Obchodní dům	**ohb**-khod-nee **doom**
Grocery store	Potraviny	**poh**-trah-**vin**-ee
Pastry shop	Cukrárna	tsoo-**krar**-na
Dairy products shop	Mlekárna	mleh-**kar**-na

I would like a loaf of bread and rolls.	Chtěla bych chléb a rohlíky.	kh'**tyel**-ah bikh khleb ah **roh**-hleck-ee
Milk	Mléko	**mleh**-koh
A half kilo of this salami	Půl kilo tohoto salámu	**pool kee**-lo **toh**-ho-toh sah-**lah**-moo
This cheese	Tento sýr	**ten**-toh seer
A kilo of apples	Kilo jablek	**kee**-lo **yah**-blek
Three kilos of pears.	Tři kila hrušek.	tshree **kee**-la h'**roo**-shek
Women's clothing	Dámské odévy	**dahm**-skeh **oh**-dyeh-vee
Men's clothing	Pánské odévy	**pahn**-skeh **oh**-dyeh-vee
Souvenirs	Upomínkové předměty	**oo**-poh-**meen**-koh-veh pshed-**myeh**-tee
Toys and gifts	Hračky a dárky	h'**rahtch**-kee ah **dar**-ky
Jewelry and perfume	Bižutérie a voňavky	**bizh**-oo-teh-ree-yeh ah **voh**-nyahv-kee

At the Hotel

Room	Pokoj	**poh**-koy
I would like a room.	Chtěl (Chtěla) bych pokoj.	kh'**tyel** (kh'**tyel**-ah) bikh **poh**-koy
For one person	Pro jednu osobu	pro **yed**-noo **oh**-so-boo
For two people	Pro dvě osoby	pro dveh **oh**-so-bee
For how many nights?	Na kolik nocí?	na **ko**-lik **note**-see
For tonight	Na dnešní noc	na **dnesh**-nee notes
For two nights	Na dvě nocí	na dveh **note**-see
For a week	Na týden	na **tee**-den
Do you have a different room?	Máte jiný pokoj?	**ma**-teh **yee**-nee **poh**-koy
With a bath	S koupelnou	s'**ko**-pel-noh
With a shower	Se sprchou	seh **sp'r**-kho
With a toilet	S toaletou	s'twa-**leh**-to
The key, please.	Klíc, prosím.	kleech **pro**-seem
How much is it?	Kolik to stojí?	**ko**-lik toh **stoy**-ee
My bill, please.	Účet, prosím.	**oo**-chet **pro**-seem

Czech Vocabulary

Dining Out

Café	Kavárna	ka-**vahr**-na
Restaurant	Restaurace	res-toh-**vrat**-seh
A table for two	Stůl pro dva	stool pro dvah
Waiter, the menu, please.	Pane vrchní! Jídelní lístek, prosím.	**pah**-neh **verkh**-nee **yee**-dell-nee **lis**-tek **pro**-seem
The wine list, please.	List vin, prosím. (or, vinny lístek).	leest vin **pro**-seem **vin**-nee **lis**-tek
The main course	Hlavní jídlo	**hlav**-nee **yid**-lo
What would you like?	Co si přejete?	tso see **psheh**-yeh-teh
What would you like to drink?	Co se přejete k pití?	tso seh **psheh**-yeh-teh k'**pit**-ee
Can you recommend a good wine?	Můžete doporučit dobré víno?	**moo**-zheh-teh **doh**-por-oo-cheet **dohb**-zheh **vi**-noh
Wine, please.	Víno, prosím.	**vi**-noh **pro**-seem
Pilsner beer	Plzeňské pivo	**pil**-zen-skeh **piv**-oh
What's the specialty of the day?	Jaká je dnešní specialitá?	**ya**-ka yeh **dnesh**-nee spet-sya-lih-**tah**
I didn't order this.	Tohle jsem neobjednal.	**toh**-hleh sem **neh**-ob-yed-nahl
That's all, thanks.	Děkuji, to je všechno.	**dyek**-oo-yee to yeh **vsheh**-khno
The check, please.	Učet, prosím.	**oo**-chet **pro**-seem
Is the tip included?	Je záhrnuto zpropítně?	yeh **za**-her-noo-toh **zpro**-peet-nyeh
Enjoy your meal.	Dobrou chuť.	**doh**-broh khoot
To your health!	Na zdraví!	**na** zdrah-vee
Fork	Vidlička	**vid**-litch-ka
Knife	Nůž	noozh
Spoon	Lžíce	l'**zheet**-seh
Napkin	Ubrousek	**oo**-bro-sek
A cup of tea	Šálek čaje	**shah**-lek **tcha**-yeh
A bottle of wine	Láhev vína	**lah**-hev **vi**-nah
One beer	Jedno pivo	**yed**-noh **piv**-oh
Two beers, please.	Dvě piva, prosím.	dveh **piv**-ah **pro**-seem
Salt and pepper	Sůl a pepř	sool ah pepsh
Sugar	Cukr	**tsook**-rr

Czech Vocabulary

Bread, rolls, and butter	Chléb, rohlíky a máslo	khleb **roh**-hlee-ky ah **mah**-slo
Black coffee	Černá káva	**chair**-na **kah**-va
Coffee with milk	Káva s mlékem (or, Bílá káva)	**kah**-va s **mleh**-kem **bee**-la **kah**-va
Tea with lemon	Čaj se citrónem	tchai se **tsi**-tro-nem
Orange juice	Pomerančový džus	po-mair-**ahn**-cho-vee dzhoos
Another (masc., fem., neuter)	Ještě jeden (ještě jednu, ještě jedno)	yesh-**tyeh** ye-**den** (yesh-**tyeh** yed-**nu,** yesh-**tyeh** yed-no)
More	Ještě	yesh-**tyeh**
I'd like more mineral water.	Chtěl bych ještě minerálku.	kh'**tyel** bikh yesh-**tyeh** min-eh-**rahl**-ku
Another napkin, please.	Ještě jeden ubrousek, prosím.	yesh-**tyeh** jeh-**den** **oo**-bro-sek, **pro**-seem
More bread and butter	Ještě chléb a máslo	yesh-**tyeh** khleb ah **mah**-slo
Not too spicy	Ne příliš ostré	neh **pshee**-leesh **oh**-streh
I like the meat well done.	Chci maso dobře upečené (or, Chci propečené).	kh'tsee **mah**-so **dobe**-zheh **oo**-petch-en-eh kh'tsee **pro**-petch-en-eh
May I exchange this for . . .	Mohl bych tohle vyměnit za . . .	**mole** bikh **to**-hleh **vee**-myen-it zah

At the Airport

Airport	Letiště	**leh**-tish-tyeh
Arrivals	Přílety	**pshee**-leh-tee
Where are the taxis?	Kde jsou taxíky?	g'deh so **tak**-seek-ee
Is there a subway?	Je tady metro?	yeh **tah**-dee **meh**-tro
Is there a bus?	Je tady autobus?	yeh **tah**-dee **out**-oh-boos
Stop here, please!	Zastavte tady, prosím!	**zah**-stahv-teh **tah**-dee pro-seem
What is the fare to downtown?	Kolik to stojí do středu města?	**ko**-lik toh **stoy**-ee doh st'**shreh**-doo **myes**-tah
Have a good trip!	Šťastnou cestu!	sht'**shast**-no **tsest**-oo

Czech Vocabulary

At the Post Office

Post office	Pošta	**po**-shta
Stamps, please.	Známky, prosím.	**znahm**-kee **pro**-seem
For letters or for postcards?	Na dopisy nebo na pohlednice?	na **doh**-pis-ee **neh**-bo poh-**hled**-nit-seh
To where are you mailing the letters?	Kam posíláte dopisy?	kahm **poh**-see-**lah**-teh **doh**-pis-ee
To the United States	Do Spojených Států	doh **spoy**-en ikh **stah**-too
Airmail	Letecky	**leh**-tet-skee
The telephone directory	Telefonní seznam	te-le-**fon**-nee **sez**-nahm
Where can I go to make a telephone call?	Odkud mohu telefonovat?	**ohd**-kood **moh**-hoo te-le-**fo**-no-**vaht**
A telephone call	Telefonní rozhovor	te-le-**fon**-nee **rohz**-ho-vor
A collect call	Hovor na účet volaného	**ho**-vor na **oo**-chet **voh**-lah-**neh**-ho
What number, please?	Jaké číslo, prosím?	**yah**-keh **chee**-slo **pro**-seem
May I speak to Mrs. Newton, please.	Mohl bych mluvit s paní Newtonovou. prosím.	**mole** bikh **mloo**-vit **spah**-nee **new**-ton-oh-voh **pro**-seem
The line is busy.	Je obsázeno.	yeh ob-**sah**-zen-**oh**
There's no answer.	Nehlásí se.	**neh**-hlah-see seh
Try again later.	Zkuste to pozdějí.	**zkoo**-steh toh po-**zdyay**-ee
May I leave a message, please?	Mohla bych nechát vzkaz, prosím?	**moh**-hla **bikh** **neh**-khaht v'**zkahz** **pro**-seem

INDEX

✕ = restaurant, 🏨 = hotel

A

Adidas (shop), 79
AghaRTA (jazz club), 71
AghaRTA International Jazz Festival, 6
Airports and airlines, *xvii–xviii, xxiv*
All Saints' Chapel, 50
Antikvariát Karel Křenek (shop), 78
Antiques shops, 78
Apartments and private rooms, 63
Apollo 🏨, 68
Arcibiskupský palác, 37
Art galleries and museums
Hrdčany, 36, 38
Prague Castle, 45, 48
Art Program (shop), 78
Astra 🏨, 68
Astronomical clock, 12, 19
ATMs, *xix, xxvii–xxviii*
AVE (tourist service), 63
Axa 🏨, 65

B

Balkan 🏨, 69
Ballet, 74–75
Bars, 71–72
Bazilika svatého Jiří, 43
Bella Napoli ✕, 58
Belmondo Revival Club, 72
Belvedere, 49
Bethlehem Chapel, 13–14
Betlémská kaple, 13–14
Bílá Labut' (department store), 77
Bistro Bruncvík, 33
Bohemia (shop), 79
Bohemian Chancellery, 49–50
Book shops, 78
Brahe, Tycho, 21
Bretfeld Palác, 27–28
Buquoy Palace, 33
Bus travel, *xxii, xxx*

C

Cabarets, 71
Capriccio (shop), 79
Car travel, *xxii–xxiii, xxx–xxxi*
Castle District, 35–39
Čedok, *xxi, xxiii, xxvi*
Celetná ulice, 12, 14
Cemeteries, 22–23, 24–25, 42
Cerberus ✕, 58
Ceremony Hall, 23
Černínský palác, 36, 37
Česká kancelář, 49–50
Česka Národní banka, 9
Chapel of St. Válav (Wenceslas), 46
Chapel of the Holy Cross, 45
Charles Bridge, 26–35
Chernin Palace, 36, 37
Children's shops, 79
Chrám svatého Mikuláše, 27, 28
Chrám svatého Víta, 42, 45–48
Churches
concerts in, 73–74
Hrdčany, 36, 37
Malá Strana, 27, 28, 30–31
Old Town, 12, 13–14, 15–16, 20–21
Prague Castle, 42, 43, 45–48
Vinohrady, 41
Church of Our Lady of Perpetual Help at the Theatines, 28
Church of Our Lady Victorious, 30–31
Church of St. Giles, 13, 15
Church of St. James, 74
Church of St. John Nepomuk, 36
Church of St. Nicholas, 12, 15–16, 73
Church of St. Procopius, 27
Church of Sts. Simon and Jude, 73–74
Church of the Most Sacred Heart, 41
City Hotel Moráň, 65
City of Prague Accommodation Service, 63
Clam-Gallas palota, 13, 14
Climate, 5–6
Clock towers, 19
Corona Club and Latin Café, 71
Costs, *xxvii*
Council chamber, 50

Crown Chamber, 47
Crypts, 47
Crystal shops, 78–79
Currency, *xxvii*
Customs, *xxiv–xxv*
Czech National Bank, 9
Czech National Gallery, 48
Czech National Museum, 9
Czech Tourist Authority, *xxiii*

D

Defenestration, *18*, 49–50
Department stores, 77
Diplomat 🏨, 64
Discos, 71
Doctors, *xix*
Dolly Bell ✕, 58
Duties, *xxiv–xxv*
Dvořák Hall, 73

E

Embassies, *xviii*
Emergencies, *xviii–xix*
Estates Theater, *9*, *20*, 74–75
Exchanging money, *xxvii*

F

Fakhreldine ✕, 55
Festival of 20th Century Music, 6
Festivals, 6
Film, 73
Food shops, 79
Fruits de France (shop), 79

G

Garden on the Ramparts, 73
Gardens
Letna, 40
Malá Strana, *27*, *34*, 35
Prague Castle, 48–49
Gay travel, *xix*
Globe Bookstore and Coffeehouse, 78
Golden Lane, 52
Gottwald, Klement, 17
Government tourist offices, *xxiii*
Granát (shop), 79
Grand Hotel Bohemia, 64
Grand Priory Square, 33
Guided tours, *xxvi*

H

Harmony 🏨, 65
Havelská ulice, 77
Health, *xix*, *xxvi*
Hello Ltd. (tourist service), 63
High Synagogue, *22*, 25
Holešovice, 39–40
Holešovice (flea market), 77
Holidays, *xxviii*
Holocaust memorials, 23
Hosteling, *xx*
Hotel Europa, *9*, 15
Hotel Paříž, 17
Hotels, 4–5, 64–69
Houses, historic
Malá Strana, *32*, 33
Prague Castle, 52
Hradčanské náměstí, *36*, 37
Hradčany, 35–39
Hus, Jan, 15
Hussites, *18*, 29

I

"Infant of Prague," 27
Insurance, *xix*

J

James Joyce Pub, 72
Jan Hus monument, *12*, 15
Jazz clubs, 71
Jewelry shops, 79
Jewish Ghetto, 22–25
Jewish Town Hall, *22*, 25
John of Nepomuk, St., 47–48
Jo's Bar, 72
Josefov, 22–25, 77

K

Kafka, Franz, *17*, *33*, 52
birthplace, *12*, 14
grave, 42
Kampa 🏨, 65
Kampa Island and Gardens, *27*, 28–29
Kaple svatého Kříže, 45
Karlova ulice, *12*, *15*, 77
Karlův most, *26*, 29–30
Karmelitská, 27
Kinský Palace, *12*, 17
Klášter svatého Jiří, 48

Index

Kogo Pizzeria-Caffeteria, 55
Kostel Nejsvětějšího Srdce Páně, 41
Kostel Panny Marie před Týnem, 12, 20–21
Kostel Panny Marie ustavičné pomoci u Kajetánů, 28
Kostel Panny Marie vítězné, 27, 30–31
Kostel svatého Jana Nepomuckého, 36
Kostel svatého Jiljí, 13, 15
Kostel svatého Martina ve zdi, 13, 15
Kostel svatého Mikuláše, 12, 15–16
Kotva (department store), 79
Královský letohrádek, 49
Královský palác, 42, 49–50
Královská zahrada, 48–49
Krone (department store), 77, 79
Kundera, Milan, 30

L

Language, xxvi, 80–87
Laterna Magika, 75
Lávka (disco), 71
Lennon Peace Wall, 31
Letenské sady, 40
Letná, 39–40
Libraries, 39
Little Quarter, 26–35
Little Quarter Square, 31
Lobkovická ✕, 59–60
Lobkovický palác, 50–51, 74
Loew, Rabbi, 25
Loreto Church, 36, 37
Lounges, 71–72
Lucerna Bar, 71

M

Magic Theater of the Baroque World, 75
Mail service, xxvi
Maislova synagóga, 23
Malá Strana, 26–35
Malá Strana bridge towers, 26, 31
Malé náměstí, 12, 16
Malostranska Beseda (rock club), 72
Malostranské náměstí, 27, 31
Maltézské náměstí, 27, 31

Martinický palác, 36
Matyášova brána, 51
Melodia (shop), 79
Mepro ✕, 68–69
Merchants' Bank, 9, 21–22
Meteor Plaza ✕, 65, 68
Metro, xxxi
Military History Museum, 38
Monasteries, 38–39
Money, xix, xxvii–xxviii
"Monuments of the Czech National Past" (exhibition), 50–51
Morzin Palace, 32
Moser (shop), 78–79
Mostecká ulice, 26
Mostecká věž, 26
Mozart, W. A., 28, 34–35, 37
Municipal House, 12, 16–17
Museum of National Literature, 39
Museums
in Hradčany, 36, 38, 39
Jewish culture, 22, 25
in Josefov, 22, 25
Kafka, 14
literature, 39
military, 38
modern art, 40
Mozart, 34–35
National Museum, 9
in Old Town, 14, 16
Music, 73–74
Musical instrument shops, 79
Myslivna ✕, 60

N

Náměstí Republiky, 9, 16
Na příkopě, 9, 16
Národní divadlo, 74
Národní galérie, 36, 38
Národní Muzeum, 9
Národní třída, 9, 13, 77
National Boulevard, 13
National Gallery, 36, 38
National Marionette Theater, 75
National Theater, 74
Na Zvonařce ✕, 58–59
Nerudova ulice, 27, 32, 36, 77
New Jewish Cemetery, 42
Nightlife, 71–72
Nový Svět, 36, 38

Index

O

Obchod Všim Možným (shop), 79
Obecní dům, 12, 16–17, 73
Obřadní síň, 23
Obrazárna, 45
Office buildings, 16
Old Castle Steps, 51
Old Jewish Cemetery, 22–23, 24
Old-New Synagogue, 22, 24
Old Town, 9, 12–22
Old Town Bridge Tower, 26, 33
Old Town Hall, 12, 18–19
Old Town Square, 12, 18
Opening and closing times, xxviii
Opera, 74–75
Opera ⛨, 69

P

Palace ⛨, 64
Palaces
Hrdčany, 37
Malá Strana, 27–28, 33, 34, 35
Old Town, 14, 17
Prague Castle, 49–51
Palác Kinských, 12, 17
Památník národního písemnictví, 39
Pařížská Street, 24, 77
Parks
Letenské sady, 40
Malá Strana, 27, 34
Parnas ✕, 58
Passports, xx, xxviii
Penguin's ✕, 61
Pension Louda, 69
Pension Unitas, 69
Pension U Raka, 68
Personal guides, xxvi
Petřín, 39
Pezinok ✕, 59
Pharmacies, xix
Philosophical Hall, 39
Picture Gallery, 45
Piano Bar, 72
Pinkasova synagóga, 23, 24
Pizzeria Coloseum, 59
Plane travel
airports and airlines, xvii, xxiv
between airport and downtown, xvii–xviii
from North America, xvii
from United Kingdom, xvii

Pohořelec, 36, 38
Porcelain shops, 78–79
Potomac ✕, 54–55
Powder Tower, 9, 17–18
Prague Autumn International Music Festival, 6
Prague Castle, 42–52
Druhé nádvoří (Second Courtyard), 43
První nádvoří (First Courtyard), 51
Třetí nádvoří (Third Courtyard), 52
Prague City of Music Festival, 6
Prague Information Service, xxiii
Prague International Film Festival, 6
Prague Marathon, 6
Prague Spring Music Festival, 6
Prague Summer Culture Festival, 6
Prague Writers' Festival, 6
Prašná brána, 9, 17–18
Pražský Hrad. ☞ Prague Castle
Prescriptions drugs, xxvi
Profit ✕, 55
Prokopská ulice, 27
Pubs, 71–72
Puppet shows, 75

R

Radost FX (disco), 71
RC Bunkr (rock club), 72
Reduta (jazz club), 71
Republic Square, 9, 16
Restaurants, 4, 54–61
Riders' Staircase, 50
Rock Café, 72
Rock clubs, 72
Romanesque Palace, 50
Room-finding agencies, 63
Royal Garden, 48
Royal Mausoleum, 47
Royal Oratory, 47
Royal Palace, 42, 49–50
Royal Summer Palace, 49
Rusalka ✕, 59

S

St. George's Basilica, 43
St. George's Convent, 48
St. James's Church, 74
St. Martin-in-the-Wall, 13, 15
St. Nicholas Church, 27, 28, 74
St. Vitus Cathedral, 42, 45–48, 74
St. Wenceslas, statue of, 9, 19–20

Scene of Fire, 38
Schönbornský palác, 27, 33, 36
Schwarzenberský palác, 38
Senior citizens, *xx*
Shopping, 5, 77–79
Small Square, 12, 16
Specialty stores, 78–79
Sports equipment shops, 79
Stará sněmovna, 50
Staré Město. ☞ Old Town
Staré zámecké schody, 51
Staroměstská radnice, 12, 18–19
Staroměstské náměstí, 12, 18, 77
Staronová synagóga, 22, 24
Starý židovský hřbitov, 22–23, 24–25
State Jewish Museum, 22, 25
Statní Opera Praha, 74
Státní židovské muzeum, 22, 25
Stavovské divadlo, 9, 20, 74–75
Strahov 007 (rock club), 72
Strahov Library, 39
Strahovský klášter, 36, 38–39
Streetcars, *xxx*
Street markets, 77
Students, *xx*
Subway system, *xxxi*
Synagogues, 22, 23, 24

T

Taj Mahal ✕, 58
Taxis, *xxiii*, *xxxi*
Tchibo (café), 19
Telephone service, *xx*, *xxix*
Tesco (department store), 77
Theater, 75
Theater buildings, 20
Thun-Hohenstein Palace, 32
Ticket agencies, 73
Timing the visit, 5–6
Tipping, *xxix*
Tourist information, *xxiii*
Tour operators, *xxi–xxii*
Town Hall tower, 19
Train travel, *xxii*, *xxix–xxx*
Trams, *xxx*
Travel agencies, *xxiii*
Travelers with disabilities, *xviii*, *xxv*
Tržiště ulice, 27
Týn Church, 12, 20–21

U

U červeného orla, 32
U lužického semináře, 27
U Karlova Mostu (shop), 78
U Knihomola Bookstore and Café, 78
U Kocoura (café), 32
U Malého Glena (club), 72
U Mecenáše ✕, 59
U Medvídků (pub), 72
U Páva 🏨, 68
U Počtú ✕, 60
U Rychtáře ✕, 55
U tří housliček, 32
U tří pštrosů 🏨, 33, 64
U Tří Zlatých Hvězd ✕, 60
U Vejvodů (pub), 72
U zeleného čaje (café), 32
U Zlatého Tygra (pub), 72
U Zlaté Hrušky ✕, 60
U Zvonů, 12, 21

V

Václavské náměstí, 9, 21
Valkoun House, 32
Varieté Praga (nightclub), 71
Veletržni palac Museum of Modern Art, 40
Velkopřevorské náměstí, 27, 33
Villa Bertramka, 34–35, 74
Vinohrady, 41–42
Visas, *xx*, *xxviii*
Visitor information, *xxiii*, *xxxi*
V Krakovské ✕, 59
Vladislav II of Jagiello, King, 17
Vladislavský sál, 49
Vojanovy sady, 27, 34
Vojenské historické muzeum, 38
Vrtbovský palác, 30, 34
Vysoká synagóga, 22, 25
V Zátiší ✕, 55

W

Wallenstein Chapel, 48
Wallenstein Palace Gardens, 35
Weather, 5–6
Wenceslas Square, 21
Wine, 5

Z

Zahrada Valdštejnského paláca, 27, 35
Zídovské hřbitovy, 42
Zidovská radnice, 22, 25

Živnostenská banka, 9, 21–22
Zlatá ulička, 52
Zoologická Zahrada, 41
Zrcadlová Kaple, 74

Fodor's Travel Publications

Available at bookstores everywhere, or call 1-800-533-6478, 24 hours a day

Gold Guides

U.S.

Alaska
Arizona
Boston
California
Cape Cod, Martha's Vineyard, Nantucket
The Carolinas & the Georgia Coast
Chicago
Colorado
Florida
Hawai'i
Las Vegas, Reno, Tahoe
Los Angeles
Maine, Vermont, New Hampshire
Maui & Lana'i
Miami & the Keys
New England
New Orleans
New York City
Pacific North Coast
Philadelphia & the Pennsylvania Dutch Country
The Rockies
San Diego
San Francisco
Santa Fe, Taos, Albuquerque
Seattle & Vancouver
The South
U.S. & British Virgin Islands
USA
Virginia & Maryland
Washington, D.C.

Foreign

Australia
Austria
The Bahamas
Belize & Guatemala
Bermuda
Canada
Cancún, Cozumel, Yucatán Peninsula
Caribbean
China
Costa Rica
Cuba
The Czech Republic & Slovakia
Eastern & Central Europe
Europe
Florence, Tuscany & Umbria
France
Germany
Great Britain
Greece
Hong Kong
India
Ireland
Israel
Italy
Japan
London
Madrid & Barcelona
Mexico
Montréal & Québec City
Moscow, St. Petersburg, Kiev
The Netherlands, Belgium & Luxembourg
New Zealand
Norway
Nova Scotia, New Brunswick, Prince Edward Island
Paris
Portugal
Provence & the Riviera
Scandinavia
Scotland
Singapore
South Africa
South America
Southeast Asia
Spain
Sweden
Switzerland
Thailand
Tokyo
Toronto
Turkey
Vienna & the Danube

Fodor's Special-Interest Guides

Caribbean Ports of Call
The Complete Guide to America's National Parks
Family Adventures
Fodor's Gay Guide to the USA
Halliday's New England Food Explorer
Halliday's New Orleans Food Explorer
Healthy Escapes
Kodak Guide to Shooting Great Travel Pictures
Net Travel
Nights to Imagine
Rock & Roll Traveler USA
Sunday in New York
Sunday in San Francisco
Walt Disney World for Adults
Walt Disney World, Universal Studios and Orlando
Where Should We Take the Kids? California
Where Should We Take the Kids? Northeast
Worldwide Cruises and Ports of Call

Special Series

Affordables
Caribbean
Europe
Florida
France
Germany
Great Britain
Italy
London
Paris

Bed & Breakfasts and Country Inns
America
California
The Mid-Atlantic
New England
The Pacific Northwest
The South
The Southwest
The Upper Great Lakes

Berkeley Guides
California
Central America
Eastern Europe
Europe
France
Germany & Austria
Great Britain & Ireland
Italy
London
Mexico
New York City
Pacific Northwest & Alaska
Paris
San Francisco

Compass American Guides
Arizona
Canada
Chicago
Colorado
Hawaii
Idaho
Hollywood
Las Vegas
Maine
Manhattan
Montana
New Mexico
New Orleans
Oregon
San Francisco
Santa Fe
South Carolina
South Dakota
Southwest
Texas
Utah
Virginia
Washington
Wine Country
Wisconsin
Wyoming

Citypacks
Atlanta
Berline
Chicago
Hong Kong
London
Los Angeles
Montréal
New York City
Paris
Prague
Rome
San Francisco
Tokyo
Washington, D.C.

Fodor's Español
California
Caribe Occidental
Caribe Oriental
Gran Bretaña
Londres
Mexico
Nueva York
Paris

Exploring Guides
Australia
Boston & New England
Britain
California
Canada
Caribbean
China
Costa Rica
Egypt
Florence & Tuscany
Florida
France
Germany
Greek Islands
Hawai'i
Ireland
Israel
Italy
Japan
London
Mexico
Moscow & St. Petersburg
New York City
Paris
Prague
Provence
Rome
San Francisco
Scotland
Singapore & Malaysia
South Africa
Spain
Thailand
Turkey
Venice

Fodor's Flashmaps
Boston
New York
San Francisco
Washington, D.C.

Pocket Guides
Acapulco
Atlanta
Barbados
Jamaica
London
New York City
Paris
Prague
Puerto Rico
Rome
San Francisco
Washington, D.C.

Mobil Travel Guides
America's Best Hotels & Restaurants
California & the West
Frequent Traveler's Guide to Major Cities
Great Lakes
Mid-Atlantic
Northeast
Northwest & Great Plains
Southeast
Southwest & South Central

Rivages Guides
Bed and Breakfasts of Character and Charm in France
Hotels and Country Inns of Character and Charm in France
Hotels and Country Inns of Character and Charm in Italy
Hotels and Country Inns of Character and Charm in Paris
Hotels and Country Inns of Character and Charm in Portugal
Hotels and Country Inns of Character and Charm in Spain

Short Escapes
Britain
France
New England
Near New York City

Fodor's Sports
Golf Digest's Places to Play
Skiing USA
USA Today The Complete Four Sport Stadium Guide

Fodor's Vacation Planners
Great American Learning Vacations
Great American Sports & Adventure Vacations
Great American Vacations
Great American Vacations for Travelers with Disabilities
National Parks and Seashores of the East
National Parks of the West

WHEREVER YOU TRAVEL, HELP IS NEVER FAR AWAY.

From planning your trip to providing travel assistance along the way, American Express® Travel Service Offices are always there to help.

Prague

American Express Czech Republic Ltd.
Vaclavske Namesti 56
Prague
2/24 219 992

Travel

http://www.americanexpress.com/travel

American Express Travel Service Offices are found in central locations throughout Eastern Europe.

Listings are valid as of September 1996. Not all services available at all locations.
© 1996 American Express Travel Related Services Company, Inc.